Editor
Walter Kelly, M.A.

Managing Editor
Ina Massler Levin, M.A.

Editor-in-Chief
Sharon Coan, M.S. Ed.

Art Coordinator
Denice Adorno

Illustrator
Tuan Nguyen

Cover Artist
Denice Adorno

Imaging
Alfred Lau
Temo Parra

Product Manager
Phil Garcia

Publishers
Rachelle Cracchiolo, M.S. Ed.
Mary Dupuy Smith, M.S. Ed.

A Year Full of

Challenging

WRITING PROJECTS

FOR MIDDLE SCHOOL

Author

Elizabeth Whitney, Ph.D.

Teacher Created Materials, Inc.
6421 Industry Way
Westminster, CA 92683
www.teachercreated.com

©2001 Teacher Created Materials, Inc.

Made in U.S.A.

ISBN-0-7439-3256-0

Table of Contents

Introduction

A Year Full of Writing Projects for Middle School provides the teacher with planning models to use as engaging, authentic, and novel strategies to increase students' writing achievement. These writing projects have proved to be an effective strategy to meet the diverse learning needs of students. An advanced curriculum of writing activities has been integrated with differentiated instruction to increase achievement, challenge able learners, and provide an optimum curriculum for both the mixed-ability and the gifted inclusion student. Effective implementation of differentiated teaching strategies has a direct correlation with increasing student achievement.

This book provides students with a product-based curriculum that applies critical and creative thinking, student choice, expanded vocabulary development, brain-based learning, multiple intelligences approaches, and authentic assessment. A project- and product-based curriculum has shown clear evidence of increasing students' acquisition of language content skill areas. Moreover, the results show that students experience success in both the cognitive and affective domains of learning.

The writing projects in this book have become the key components of a successful, differentiated instruction program that is responsive to all students' varied readiness levels, interests, and learning profiles. Students will show increased awareness of their learning strengths and excel in the writing process. Marketing student writing strengths, student decision-making, positive self-esteem, improved writing skills, and independence with writing—these are among the priorities impacting these yearlong projects for middle school students. Students will experience achievement in skill development in all language areas through writing, speaking, listening, and reading.

Teachers will also benefit from a project-based writing curriculum that encourages the students' progressive achievement. The consistent use of individual writing conferences promotes the success of this curriculum. Writing conference guidelines have been supplied to help teachers increase the positive effects of using individual writing conferences to identify deficiencies and build writing proficiency. The writing conferences have a significant increase on student achievement. Through these conferences, the students will learn to self-correct and write clearly and effectively. They will be able to pre-write, draft, revise, edit, and publish all assigned work. The students will learn how to transfer skill building of grammar, punctuation, and spelling into their own writing. The students also will acquire the ability to evaluate their work. The writing projects are engaging, students are protected from initial failure, and student participation is 100%.

This book provides the tools for students to combine pride, talent, persistence, creativity, novelty, variety, and depth through their writing. The students will witness excellence with their own eyes, achieved through writing as a powerful means of communicating who they are while exploring the discovery and potential for their future.

Writing rubrics have been provided for students and teachers for assessment of the writing projects assigned. An additional writing conference rubric has been supplied to guide students in improvement through self-evaluation.

A helpful listing of transitions, "dead" words, sensory words, and synonyms has been included (on pages 10–16) to reproduce for students to place in their spiral notebooks and use as an essential tool to initiate higher standards in sentence structure, eliminate common and overused words, and increase vocabulary choice. Encourage students to refer to this listing, along with using a thesaurus or other reference, before writing the final draft for any activity.

Introduction *(cont.)*

Teacher Benefits

The teacher identifies and encourages students' learning potential, using differentiated writing instruction concurrently with the multiple intelligences theory. In addition, by using teacher-directed, individual writing conferences that focus on developing each student's writing strengths, the teacher can use appropriate individualized instruction to address each student's writing weakness.

Writing conferences eliminate taking papers home to correct. All correction is done in class, and students write the final drafts at home. Class time is used for instruction and writing rough drafts. The teacher will be able to use curriculum compacting to avoid teaching skills which have been previously taught.

With the use of staggered writing conferences, the student may work at his particular writing pace, which will result in a higher quality product. The teachers' role as a facilitator and motivator becomes a positive effect on student performance. The teacher thus creates an atmosphere that is non-threatening.

The integration of language arts and technology is emphasized and encouraged. Writing across the curriculum is utilized with block scheduling of core classes and team teaching. The use of student-selected themes, thus guaranteeing student interest, creates a positive attitude about writing. Novelty and variety engage the students' attention as they create their own products. Students work individually on their projects but share and brainstorm together to extend and expand creative and critical thinking. The teacher observes the continuous writing progress of students as they learn to apply writing conventions, sentence combining, spelling, and expanded vocabulary usage. Teachers witness students who have the opportunity to use creative and critical thinking while exploring brain-based learning. Teachers experience personal success from the projects taught, which builds self-confidence for the teacher and the student in future writing assignments.

Student Benefits

Students are able to discover and market their learning strengths, which increases their focus on writing as a positive experience. Successful writing experiences promote positive self-esteem. Writing skills improve with a student-generated project. Students show independence with writing, become more motivated, and are active self-starters with writing. Students are able to transfer knowledge directly to their writing while simultaneously being able to work at their own pace. Since the class is student-centered, they choose to work collaboratively and/or independently. Ongoing self-assessment of rough drafts means they will be checking spiral notebooks weekly for work completed. All students keep track of assigned and completed work. All students are capable of completing this project. These projects are set up for nonfailure. Student ownership is the key to these successful writing projects.

Writing Rubric

Use the following rubric to assess students' writing projects. If you prefer, create your own rubric or work with students to create a joint rubric for project evaluation and assessment.

Exceptional (6)

❑ Student clearly describes the writing situation in multiple paragraphs, using appropriate and varied transitions.

❑ The writer displays a rich, vivid vocabulary and does not use any "dead" words.

❑ The writer uses a well-developed topic sentence and sequential supporting details.

❑ The writer includes setting, development of the topic, and a sound conclusion.

❑ The writer addresses the specific type of writing style with the knowledge of expectations, using vivid language, advanced sentence structure, and correct grammar, spelling, and punctuation.

❑ The student's writing demonstrates creative and critical thinking, revealing depth, complexity, and novelty.

Strong (5)

❑ The student describes the writing situation in multiple paragraphs, using repeated transitions in a well-developed paragraph.

❑ The student uses no "dead" words.

❑ The student demonstrates full understanding of the topic assigned.

❑ The topic sentence and supporting details are written sequentially.

❑ The student exhibits the ability to write a conclusion summarizing his or her point of view.

❑ The student demonstrates some variety in sentence structure, uses some vivid words, and commits few grammar, punctuation, and spelling errors.

❑ The writing demonstrates the emergence of original creative and critical thinking, revealing depth, complexity, and novelty.

Writing Rubric *(cont.)*

Competent (4)

❏ The student describes the writing situation in multiple paragraphs, using repeated transitions and few dead words. The topic sentence and supporting sentences are informing, but ordinary.

❏ The paragraphs have common language with little use of vivid language.

❏ The writing assignment is understood, but only average effort is exhibited.

❏ There are some spelling, punctuation, and grammar errors.

❏ Complete sentences are written with little variety in sentence structure.

❏ Some creativity and critical thinking are demonstrated.

Developing (3)

❏ The student describes the writing situation in one paragraph. The student may have only a limited understanding of the writing task assigned.

❏ The paragraph is partially developed with restricted details.

❏ There are run-on sentences and fragments. The writing has spelling, punctuation, and grammar errors. The conclusion is simplified.

❏ Slight demonstration of creative and critical thinking or depth, complexity, and novelty exists in the writing.

Limited (2)

❏ The writing is missing major components in paragraph development.

❏ The writing consists of run-on sentences, fragments, and multiple spelling, punctuation, and sentence structure errors.

❏ The task completed has major flaws in the writing process and does not address the writing assignment.

❏ The work was done quickly and carelessly.

❏ The writing demonstrates no creative or critical thinking, failing to display depth, complexity, and novelty.

Emerging (1)

❏ The writing is incomplete.

❏ The writing displays no effort or understanding of the assignment.

❏ Errors in grammar, punctuation, and spelling dominate the task.

❏ Run-on sentences and fragments make the writing difficult to read and understand.

❏ The student failed to stay on the subject of the assignment.

Writing Conferences

Tips

As each article is taught, allow the students to write at their own pace. Conducting individual writing conferences on each article is suggested. Before conferencing, remind the students to proofread each article. Provide a private setting for each student writing conference. These conferences are to be used for student self-correction.

✏ The teacher facilitates the writing conferences. During the conference, have the student read aloud what has been written. The student is expected to make all corrections with his pen, as guided by the teacher through the writing conference. If there is a convention error, prod the student to analyze where the correction is needed. For example, when the student has problems with comma punctuation, the teacher may ask the student to read the sentence aloud again (if it is an appropriate example) so the student might hear where the comma belongs.

✏ If careless spelling or convention errors are noticed, the student will be requested to return, proofread, correct, and reschedule the next conference. This encourages students to become more competent with writing and proofreading. Since the writing process for students is varied, the teacher uses this time to be able to stagger scheduled student conferences.

✏ A high expectation for the student to proofread carefully is established early at the beginning of each project. This keeps the student aware that he or she is the responsible party in the use of proper spelling, accurate syntax, and correct writing conventions.

✏ The student and teacher will be able to see individual writing weaknesses since skill level varies from student to student. Curriculum compacting of skills that have been previously taught is utilized. Review time for isolated skill teaching is limited and used only during conferencing.

✏ In-class writing conferences budget the teacher's time for correcting work with each student, so the student is able to understand how to transfer writing skills that have been taught to the project being developed.

✏ A higher quality final product results from conferencing with each student. Primarily, this is because the student has already completed the major correcting. Therefore, the teacher can quickly skim over the final draft and grade the project since all the rough drafts have been read, corrected, revised, and rewritten for final copies.

Writing Conferences *(cont.)*

The writing portion of each project can be assessed through individual writing conferences. Each student should meet with the teacher individually and read the rough draft of his or her project. The student and the teacher use the guidelines below to improve writing proficiency before revising all final copies. Questions each student will answer include the following:

1. What do you like best about this project?
2. What selections need revisions?
3. What articles would benefit by choosing more advanced vocabulary words?
4. Would proofreading your selections more carefully eliminate any careless errors in spelling and punctuation?

Evaluation Guidelines

	Voice	Word Choice	Content	Organization	Sentence Fluency	Conventions
4	The writer speaks directly to the reader in a way that shows creative and original thought.	Word choices convey a real effort in expanded vocabulary usage. The writing has depth with full, rich language choices.	The project shows critical and creative thinking through the entire writing process.	The organization of the selection shows depth, variety, and novelty.	The student's writing flows well when read aloud.	The writer demonstrates a strong command of correct grammar and convention usage during paragraph development.
3	The writer shows ownership, confidence, and purpose.	The writing displays several instances of expanded vocabulary usage, mixed with a few common word choices.	The project keeps the reader's attention with several creative selections.	The order and structure of selections show correct syntax with appropriate topic sentences and supporting detail.	Sentences are generally well constructed without run-ons and fragments.	The writer demonstrates a basic command of correct grammar and convention usage during paragraph development.
2	The writer seems sincere but shows only basic knowledge of the topic.	The writing selection displays only a few instances of expanded vocabulary usage.	Development of the writing selections shows average effort, and the writing selections have been followed and completed.	The writer uses ordinary organization.	Sentences tend to be mechanical.	The writing contains a few misusages of grammar and writing conventions.
1	The product is acceptable but shows average effort.	The writing selection consists almost entirely of common, frequently used words.	The writing selection shows common and ordinary ideas.	The organization of the selection creates confusion for the reader.	Common sentences frequent the writing selection.	The writing contains several grammatical errors and misusages of writing conventions.

Tips for Teacher Guides

◆ Each student must have a spiral notebook. A large spiral notebook may be used for the entire year. The notebook will be used only for rough-draft work done in class. Students must bring their spiral notebooks to class daily. Students have fewer problems losing their work when it is accessible in one notebook. All final copies will be word-processed or handwritten in ink at home.

◆ Student Guide sheets—project assignments, check-off lists, outlines, transitions, sensory words, synonyms, and dead word lists—should be stapled or glued inside the spiral notebooks. The loss of any student-guide material will result in clean-up time during break or at the end of the class period. This saves the teacher time from duplicating additional material, and students become more responsible with their assignment sheets.

◆ Dictionaries and thesaurus use is mandatory for increased vocabulary and spelling proficiency. A class set of both is recommended. All students are responsible for self-correcting all spelling errors. Remind the students that the spell-check on computers does not respond to incorrect homonym usage.

◆ The integration of technology is encouraged with every project. The availability of computers to some students may be limited. Encourage word processing as much as possible. Several students may work ahead with the option of using school computers to word process final copies. The combination of original art work and computer graphics should be student choice. Several students will show extensive talent as recognized artists.

◆ Student samples have been supplied as writing models in order to show final products. The student samples have been collected from 6th grade classes to expose the creativity, depth, novelty, and complexity in student writing.

◆ The time frame suggested may vary for each project taught. For the highest quality work, student productivity with each class project must remain flexible.

◆ The writing projects have been organized according to degree of difficulty and time frame. Skill development in complete sentence structure with correct use of present tense verbs, past tense verbs, past participles, and homonyms precedes the more complex writing projects, which eventually include all eight writing styles.

◆ The writing projects may be used as a portfolio and an articulation and assessment tool for curriculum previously taught; future student needs in language arts content areas can then be assessed.

Transitions

Key words called *transitions* are the signals a good writer uses to show the order in which things happened. Transitional words help the reader move from idea to idea by stating or implying the connection between ideas. Transitions keep the reader focused on the order of events or thoughts. Following are some groupings of frequently used transitional words and phrases you may wish to use.

Words That Show Sequence and Time

after	next	before
during	earlier	later
at the same time	while	last
first, second, third, etc.	meanwhile	simultaneously

Words That Link Thoughts

again	also	and
so	besides	further
furthermore	in addition	last
likewise	moreover	next

Words That Compare Ideas

also	as well as	in the same way
likewise	similarly	resembling

Words That Contrast Ideas

after all	although	even though
however	nevertheless	on the contrary
on the other hand	yet	

Words That Show Cause and Effect

accordingly	due to	therefore
consequently	then	as a result
since	thus	because

Words That Emphasize

definitely	certainly	indeed
in fact	surely	to be sure
truly	undoubtedly	without a doubt

Words That Summarize

consequently	to sum up	in conclusion
in closing	finally	ultimately

Dead Words

Some words in the English language tend to be overused and, therefore, lose their power. These are called *dead words*. Below is a list of dead words and some interesting alternatives. You may wish to add others to the list on a continuing basis throughout the year.

a lot, lots	numerous, heaps, many, scores, innumerable, much, a great deal, many times, often
also	too, moreover, besides, as well as, in addition to
awesome, cool, rad	fine, wonderful, marvelous, fantastic, excellent
awful	dreadful, alarming, frightful, terrible, horrid, shocking
but	however, moreover, yet, still, nevertheless, though, although, on the other hand
fun	pleasant, pleasurable, amusing, entertaining, jolly
funny	amusing, comical, laughable, jovial, strange, peculiar, unusual
got, get	received, obtained, attained, succeed in
good	excellent, exceptional, fine, marvelous, splendid, superb, wonderful
great	wonderful, outstanding, marvelous, fantastic, excellent
guy	man, person, fellow, boy, individual
have to	need to, must
kid	child, boy, girl, youngster, youth, teen, teenager, adolescent
like	such as, similar to, similarly
mad	angry, frustrated, furious, incensed, enraged, irate
nice	pleasant, charming, fascinating, captivating, delightful, pleasurable, pleasing
pretty	attractive, comely, beautiful
scared	afraid, fearful, terrified, frightened
so	thus, accordingly, therefore
then	first, second, next, later, finally, afterward, meanwhile, soon
very	extremely, exceedingly, fantastically, unusually, incredibly, intensely, truly, fully, especially, shockingly, bitterly, immeasurably, infinitely, severely, surely, mightily, powerfully, chiefly

Sensory Words

Sensory words are those that appeal to our senses—touch, taste, smell, sight, and hearing. Using strong sensory words helps a writer convey vivid sensations to the reader by appealing to all the ways the brain can interpret meaning. Good writers always try to use strong sensory language.

Sensory Words for Describing Objects

Size/Weight

bulky	colossal	enormous	gigantic
huge	tiny	immense	massive
minute	towering	light	

Shape

broad	crooked	curved	deep
shallow	square	round	oblong
tapered	many-sided	indiscriminate	

Color

flaming	dark	bright	glowing
flashing	dull	pale	flickering
glaring	dazzling	radiant	colorful
shiny	multicolored		

Sound

thumping	squeaking	tinkling	ringing
clanging	sizzling	screeching	hissing
humming	rustling	buzzing	popping
splashing	thudding	snapping	crashing

Odor

antiseptic	burning	clean	fresh
fragrant	medicinal	musty	pungent
putrid	strong	sweet	

Texture

bumpy	crinkled	fluffy	muddy
murky	rippling	shear	wispy
cold	icy	hot	warm
smooth	rough	grainy	sandy
moist	dry	satiny	silky
velvety	oily	slippery	hairy
uneven	jagged	prickly	elastic
shaggy	cool	cuddly	greasy
tickly	gooey	gritty	slushy
earthy	lukewarm	rubbery	

Sensory Words *(cont.)*

Sensory Words for Describing Animals and People

Eyes

beady	black	blue	bright
brilliant	brown	clear	dark
dazzling	dreamy	dull	enormous
expressive	flashing	flaming	glaring
gleaming	glistening	glowing	gray
large	laughing	oval	radiant
shimmering	sparkling	starry	wide

Stature/Body Build

bent	big	bulky	chubby
colossal	crooked	enormous	fat
gigantic	graceful	grotesque	heavy
huge	immense	large	light
little	long	massive	minute
petite	portly	short	skinny
small	stout	tall	thin
tiny	towering	lanky	gangling

Hair/Body Covering

bald	black	blonde	brown
brunette	coarse	crinkled	curly
dark	feathered	fluffy	fuzzy
glistening	golden	green	gray
long	multicolored	red	scaly
short	smooth	spotted	straight
thick	white	yellow	

Complexion

black	blushing	dark	light
pale	radiant	rosy	ruddy
tan	white	wizened	blotchy

Personality

bold	ferocious	fierce	generous
gentle	happy	kingly	mean
shy	sly	vicious	kind

Sensory Words *(cont.)*

Sensory Words for Describing Settings

Weather

balmy	breezy	cold	cool
damp	dusty	dry	foggy
frosty	hazy	hot	humid
murky	rainy	starry	steamy
stormy	sunny	warm	wet
windy			

Sounds

babbling	banging	bark	bawl
bellowing	blaring	blasting	bleat
booming	bumping	buzzing	cackle
cheering	chiming	clamoring	clanging
clapping	clashing	coo	crackling
crashing	crook	crunching	cry
deafening	echoing	exploding	groan
growl	gurgling	hiss	hissing
hoot	howl	howling	humming
inaudible	jingling	jangling	lapping
loud	noisy	patter	peal
peep	popping	purr	quiet
raging	raspy	raucous	reverberating
ringing	roaring	rowdy	rumbling
rustling	scream	screech	screeching
shrill	silence	sizzling	sloshing
snapping	snarl	snort	splashing
squared	squeaking	still	swishing
thudding	thumping	thundering	tinkling
tolling	tweet	uproar	wail
whimpering	whine	whispering	whistling
working	yelling	zinging	

Odors

antiseptic	burning	clean	earthy
fragrant	fresh	gaseous	medicinal
moldy	musty	piney	pungent
rotten	smoky	stagnant	stale
strong	sweet		

Sensory Words *(cont.)*

Sensory Words for Describing Food

Taste			
biting	bittersweet	bland	burnt
buttery	creamy	crisp	delicious
fishy	flavorful	fruity	gingery
grainy	hearty	hot	juicy
mild	minty	nutty	oily
peppery	salty	savory	smooth
sour	spicy	strong	sugary
sweet	tangy	tart	tasteless
tasty	vinegary	zesty	

Texture			
bubbly	chewy	cold	crunchy
dry	gooey	grainy	gritty
hard	hot	icy	moist
oily	rough	slick	slimy
smooth	soft	sticky	waxy

Odor			
apples	bacon	freshly baked bread	sweet
bakery-like	cinnamon	delicious	fishy
fresh	meaty	pungent	salty
savory	smoky	sour	spicy
strong			

Synonyms

Synonyms are words that mean the same or nearly the same thing. Synonyms allow good writers to express shades of meaning, and thus their writing becomes sharper and more accurate than it otherwise might be. Among the most frequently and commonly used words in English are the verbs *said*, *go*, and *make*. Notice the wide variety of synonyms below that you may occasionally substitute for those verbs in order to express your meaning more accurately.

Said

acknowledged	added	admitted	advised
agreed	announced	answered	approved
argued	asked	assumed	assured
babbled	bargained	began	boasted
bragged	called	claimed	commanded
commented	complained	cried	decided
demanded	denied	described	dictated
emphasized	estimated	exclaimed	expressed
feared	giggled	grunted	indicated
insisted	laughed	lectured	lied
mentioned	moaned	mumbled	murmured
nagged	noted	notified	objected
observed	ordered	pleaded	pointed out
prayed	predicted	questioned	reassured
related	repeated	replied	requested
responded	restated	revealed	roared
ruled	scolded	screamed	shouted
shrieked	snapped	sneered	sobbed
spoke	sputtered	stammered	stated
stormed	suggested	taunted	thought
told	urged	uttered	vowed
wailed	warned	whispered	

Go

amble	arrive	chase	crawl
enter	fall	float	fly
glide	hope	jump	leap
leave	lurch	plunge	ride
run	skip	slide	soar
spin	stagger	stride	stroll
travel	tumble	twirl	walk

Make

blend	build	carve	color
construct	copy	cut	draw
fix	form	mix	mold
pour	repair	stir	stuff
tear	prepare		

Pest Patrol Wanted Poster

Teacher Guide

Objectives: Jump start your students' descriptive writing by emphasizing the use of complete sentences, vivid language, and present tense verbs in a creative writing project. This poster will be displayed in the classroom to further support student affirmation. This project promotes imagination, humor, and skill development with writing enjoyment.

Time Frame: three to four days

Materials: spiral notebook, construction paper, ruler, markers, colored pencils, tagboard, dictionary, thesaurus

Directions

- Read aloud the student check-off list on page 19 for the Pest Patrol Wanted Poster.
- Ask students to think of any additional annoying pests. Brainstorm about unusual annoyances— some can merely be exaggerated versions of daily occurrences. Explain to the students that there are no wrong answers.
- Students should be encouraged to draw their creatures first before they write their descriptions. Computer graphics may also be added.

Writing Directions: Students must write vivid topic sentences. Remind them to keep their transitions paper out to avoid dead words and increase their variety in sentence structure. Using the student check-off list, students may choose all of the requirements and add some of their own. Suggest sequential description from head to toe. Only complete sentences will be acceptable; students may not simply list characteristics. This encourages descriptive writing with complete sentence structure, vivid adjectives, and action verbs. Verbs must be kept in present tense. By using a thesaurus or dictionary, the class may together develop a word bank of action verbs and vivid adjectives that may be written on the board. The students may transfer these words into their spiral notebooks. Also, before beginning their rough drafts, students should check a thesaurus for additional descriptive words that may help develop their pest's description.

Writing Conferences: Allow brief writing conferences with each student to begin assessing individual student needs, as well as the writing ability of the class.

Art Work: Students may need to sketch their pests in pencil in their spiral notebooks. The poster must be colorful to display in the classroom. Each pest should cover the surface of a standard size sheet of construction paper. Students are encouraged to type a final draft of their description and glue it onto their wanted poster.

Due Date: On the due date, students will be eager to volunteer and read their Pest Patrol Wanted Poster in front of the class.

Grading: As the student is reading the poster aloud, the grading may take place during the presentation using the rubric on pages five and six. The writing conferences will have provided the content and conventions usage for previous assessment.

Display: After students have read their descriptions and shown their posters, they may be allowed to choose where they would like the posters to be displayed.

Pest Patrol Wanted Poster *(cont.)*

Student Guide

Name: _____

Date Due: _____

Materials: spiral notebook, construction paper, ruler, markers, colored pencils, tagboard, dictionary, thesaurus

Directions: You have been hired as a secret agent by the F.B.I., the C.I.A., and the X-Files because you have seen a creature only you can identify! These creatures are so mysterious that students are the only people who are alert enough to actually see them commit their annoying pranks. The pranks that these creatures commit are just mischievous actions to annoy you and others. For example, these creatures take peanuts out of Snickers bars just when you are ready to take your first bite. Also, just as you sit down to taste your buttery popcorn, the butter has suddenly disappeared. These pests have also been known to take the bubbles out of bubble gum!

Your job, as a special agent, is to draw this annoying creature with complete detail from head to toe. Include all its physical characteristics since it is not human.

Remember, it is not violent and doesn't carry any weapons—it is just annoying and a pest! The wanted poster must be in color to help other students to be on the watch. The pest must be captured alive!

First, begin by drawing your creature in detail in your spiral notebook. Use the description requirements on page 19 to give you ideas for describing this annoying pest. As soon as you have drawn your rough draft, redraw it on a piece of construction paper. Make it colorful! After the picture is finished, begin writing your description in complete sentences. Use the best descriptive words you can find in your dictionary, thesaurus, and from the word bank already written in your spiral notebook. The better the description, the better the chance this pest will be caught. Glue your description under your picture. These wanted posters will be displayed throughout the classroom, just in case some fellow student may want the reward! Good Luck! Happy Hunting!

Reminder: All you need is your imagination!

18

Pest Patrol Wanted Poster *(cont.)*

Student Guide

Check-Off List

The following is a list of questions to be answered in your description of the pests.

- ❏ What name is this pest known by?
- ❏ What is this creature wanted for?
- ❏ What is its approximate height and weight?
- ❏ Does it have an unusual skin color and texture?
- ❏ What type of costume, clothes, or disguise does it wear?
- ❏ Does it have unusual facial hair?
- ❏ Does it have any animal traits?
- ❏ What is its hair color and hairstyle?
- ❏ Is this creature hairless?
- ❏ How does this creature walk?
- ❏ Does this creature fly?
- ❏ Does this creature crawl?
- ❏ Does it have hands and feet?
- ❏ What kind of language does it use?
- ❏ Does it have any distinguishing marks, like scars or tattoos?
- ❏ What time of the day does it perform its annoying pranks?
- ❏ Where does it hide out?
- ❏ What would be the safest way to catch this creature?
- ❏ What kind of harmless trap could you set in order to save the public from its annoying pranks?
- ❏ What reward is offered for capturing it alive?
- ❏ What telephone number should be called if another student sees this creature?

Word Bank of Descriptive Adjectives and Action Verbs

1. _____
2. _____
3. _____
4. _____
5. _____
6. _____
7. _____
8. _____
9. _____
10. _____

11. _____
12. _____
13. _____
14. _____
15. _____
16. _____
17. _____
18. _____
19. _____
20. _____

Wanted

Spotzilla

Spotzilla is wanted for stealing the ketchup off French fries. Spotzilla weighs 152 pounds, measures five feet four inches tall, and has green skin with red spots. She has spots from her ankles to the bottom of her neck. On her arms, the spots go to her wrists. Around many people, she is an ordinary woman who has light brown skin with long black hair. On her head, there are bumps and two pieces of hair that come out of the bumps. She has hands with three fingers and feet with three toes. Spotzilla only turns into a monster when she is about to steal ketchup off French fries. Around Halloween is when she performs her annoying trick. She hides out in closets because she knows when somebody is going to have French fries, so she sneaks in and hides. While you are eating your fries and you turn your head, Spotzilla makes the ketchup disappear and reappear in front of her, and she eats it in a blink of an eye!

The safest way to catch Spotzilla is to build a steel cage at the top of all the closets near the place where you eat. Right when you are about to eat, shut all the closets and lock them, and then have all the cages fall. After a couple of minutes, open all the closets, and if any of them captured Spotzilla, call 1-800-Spotzilla immediately.

Wanted

Eardrum Buster

The creature is an extremely annoying character. It is known as the "Eardrum Buster." The Eardrum Buster is wanted because it annoys everyone at school by getting into a classroom and dragging its claws down the chalkboard.

This is what we know about it. It is approximately 8' 2" tall, weighs 200 pounds, and has a jungle-green body. It wears a belt embroidered with a yellow "M" because it belongs to the infamous Annoying Monsters Network (AMN).

It was last seen wearing blue pants, black boots that come up to its shins, and is usually shirtless and hairless as well. Its three eyes extend from its head (by about one foot) with thick antennae-like muscles. It has a nose like a pig's snout. It has a few scars from something. We are not quite sure what, but we do know it has two arms and two feet. On its hands, there are only three fingers and no thumb. With black, bat-like wings measuring about four feet across, it flies at night and is capable of penetrating school windows. It does not speak any known language and has the power to make itself invisible. It performs its pranks during school hours every school day. All that is heard is the screeching of claws dragging across the blackboard.

We have no exact location where the "Eardrum Buster" is, nor do we know where it hides out. To catch the annoying prankster, go into every classroom and put sticky sludge all over the chalkboards so that when the "Eardrum Buster" comes and tries to do its pranks, its hands will get caught in the sludge, and it won't be able to move. Then throw a net over it and call us. The reward is $4,000 for the capture of the "Eardrum Buster." We want it alive! If you see the creature, please call 1-800-BUST-EAR.

Wanted

Long-Nose George

Long-Nose George is wanted by the local peanut farmers for sucking peanuts out of their shells through his long, gigantic nose. This humongous creature weighs 500 pounds and is 6' 6" tall. The color of its unbelievably smooth skin is a dark orange. On the top of its head is a large hump growing with brown disorganized hair. The rest of its body is hairless. This creature has only three legs, which means it hops and has to crawl when he's not in human form. Although this creature has no hands, it uses its thick nose to grab things.

This disgusting creature could disguise itself as a human boy wearing dirty overalls and a tattoo of a peanut on his right leg. The tattoo is still visible on its leg when it hasn't transformed into a boy yet.

This abominable beast is amazingly grumpy and lazy! It is so lazy, it prefers to steal peanuts from one place: the farms! The peanut thief plays its annoying pranks around noon, and its hideout is at a farm.

The safest way to catch this creature is to grab a net and catch it. But beware of its hypnotizing eyes and tail of spikes. The trap I would set to save the public from this annoying creature is getting as many peanuts as I could from the farms and make a huge pit, cover it with plants, and put the peanuts on top as a decoy to persuade him to go there and fall into the pit. The reward for capturing this creature is $500,000. If anyone sees this creature, please call The Peanut Farmer Hotline at 1-800-903-0000.

Wanted

One-Armed Peggie

A creature named "One-Armed Peggie" has been sighted only once before. He is desperately wanted for stealing the aces out of every card deck in the United States. He is supposedly 12 feet 2 inches tall, weighs 8,000 pounds, and has sky-blue skin. Peggie seems to be wearing a green tank-top and tar-black Lee pants. He has no hair anywhere because the hairdo on his head is really metal. His great smelling ability can detect an ace from anywhere in the country.

He speaks no languages—at least they weren't revealed. This horrific creature gets around by the unusual jets on its legs. His most noticeable marking is a tattoo of an ace of diamonds on his chest. His hand (he has only one) is a vacuum that can take the aces out of card decks.

This very annoying creature performs his terrible crimes around the clock. He only hides out on his one day off, which is Sunday. He hides in the remote deserts of Asia. The safest way to capture this mysterious creature is to lay decks of cards all over, without the aces in them. His brain will overload, which will cause him to pass out for five minutes. The reward for capturing Peggie is one cent. As a result of this poster, you get a great chance to capture "One-Armed Peggie." Please do so! If you see him, contact me at (555) 555-5555. Thank you.

All About Me

Teacher Guide

Objectives: Teach your students about writing autobiographical incident, biography, speculation about effects, evaluation, and poetry. Reinforce the correct use of present tense, past tense, and future tense verbs with narrative writing.

This writing project is excellent for Back-to-School Night. It displays well, and students as well as parents will be able to observe writing progress from the beginning of the year. Students love to write about themselves, a circumstance that helps maintain a positive writing climate from the beginning of the year. This project also helps give the teacher a personal insight into each student.

Time Frame: four to six weeks

Materials: spiral notebook, pens, pencils, markers, colored pencils, rulers, construction paper, dictionaries, thesaurus, copies of pages 36–44

Illustrations: Illustrations may be a combination of computer graphics, photographs, and original artwork.

The Cover: Students may draw full-face or profile outlines of themselves on a blank piece of paper. Students then use magazines, newspapers, and graphics to create collages by cutting out symbols and words that best describe who they are and what they like. These symbols and words will be cut out and pasted randomly within the outline. The outline will then be cut out and pasted on the front cover of the construction paper. The outline must be completely covered. Instead of a facial outline, the full size of the cover may be used for the collage with a border containing the student's name to identify the author. Other solutions (e.g., personal snapshots) are also possible for the collage.

- This project may also be used as a holiday gift to a parent or family member.
- Students may be asked to bring in Sunday comics or wrapping paper to wrap the project.
- A holiday card may be written, designed, and added to this project.
- The project may be presented to the class with each student sharing his favorite article.

Selection One: *A Childhood Memory*

Begin this project by having students write an autobiographical incident about their earliest childhood memory. Brainstorm and share positive childhood memories. Next, write a generic topic sentence on the board to model how this incident should be written. The topic sentence states the earliest specific occurrence in the student's life. The student uses past tense verbs throughout the memory. As a class, develop a word bank of past tense verbs on the chalkboard that students may access to understand that consistent past tense usage must be followed. Many of these verbs may be transferred to their spiral notebooks as additional resources for verb choices.

Read student samples (page 25) aloud to model the writing expectation. The student samples may also be used to create an overhead transparency or be reproduced on a copier for students.

In this writing, the student should state or imply the significance of this childhood memory. The student chooses the first person point of view, and the incident should be sequential, in a chronological narrative.

This narrative has a beginning, a middle, and an end. The ending of the narrative must show the completed memory as seen through the older child's eyes.

All About Me *(cont.)*

Teacher Guide

Selection One: *A Childhood Memory*

===== **Student Sample #1: "The Kindergarten Scare"** =====

It was a week or so into the school year, and I was having a great time in kindergarten. I was playing with my friend on the jungle gym, and we were leaping off it. My friend said that I wouldn't jump off, even if my life depended on it.

Soon after, it was time to go in. I said to my friend that I would try again tomorrow. Tomorrow came like there was no night. I didn't want to go to school that day. Right when I got into class, my friend whispered to me that today was the day.

My friend was already waiting at the top of the jungle gym, just waiting for me with a terribly horrifying look on his face. I walked up the stairs, dragging my feet the whole way. As I came to the top, the drop down looked like I was staring down from the top of the Empire State Building. I was scared out of my wits. As I reached the top of the jungle gym, I crouched down. I was ready to leap like a leopard. I then saw a pole that you could slide down to the bottom. My feet had just pierced the ground, when my friend grabbed me and pulled me back to the top of the jungle gym. My friend said that it wasn't fair and that I couldn't touch anything as I went down.

I wasn't as scared that time, and I leaped right off. It felt like I touched ground before I even jumped. I still think that the jump wasn't so horrifying after all.

===== **Student Sample #2: "Stitches"** =====

The first time I got stitches was when I was five years old. My family and I went to my cousin's house on October 30th, 1993, to celebrate Halloween and eat dinner.

I was playing hide-and-seek with my cousins, my brothers, and my cousin's neighbor. It was my turn to be "it." I was told to count to fifty or something. I finished counting and said, "Ready or not, here . . ."

What I didn't realize was that standing behind me was my cousin's neighbor with a huge ball. She threw the ball and it hit me square in the back of the head. Momentum transferred from the ball to my head, and my head went flying onto a brick wall. There was a huge gash!

My parents took me to the hospital, where the doctor stuck a big needle in my head and sewed the gash together with three stitches.

I survived, and since then I have gotten stitches one other time. The great thing—or the bad thing as my brothers would say—was that I survived both incidents!

All About Me *(cont.)*

Teacher Guide

Selection Two: *An Important Person in My Life*

Students usually enjoy writing about their parents and guardians. Since some families have been combined, it is good to encourage students to write about any other family members or close relatives.

The topic sentence should include the most important people or persons in the student's life. As a class, write a generic topic sentence on the board or overhead projector. Demonstrate the use of specific supporting sentences that would be high-quality examples of expectations. Conclude the group paragraph with a strong ending that contains a reference to the topic sentence. After this activity, read or distribute copies of a student sample below to help reinforce the activity.

The student begins by using the outline in the student guide (page 38), which steers his or her writing by calling for reasons that the chosen person has such importance. The student may describe the physical, emotional, and spiritual characteristics of this person. At least three specific personality traits with examples should be included in this selection. In the conclusion, have the student restate the importance of the relationship.

━━━ Student Sample #1: "Some Important People" ━━━

Some important people really touch me in my life. First of all, my mom is always there for me and encourages me, no matter what, so I will never feel down. She never says anything negative about me or about my questions, even if they are illogical. I really approve of that. She buys me items only if I earn the privilege, not if I am irresponsible. She disciplines me only to make me a better person, not to be mean.

Secondly, I would like to write about my dad. My dad is like my mom; he disciplines me to make me a better person. For instance, if I am not disciplined, I may not discipline my own kids when I'm older. Instead of buying me toys when I am good, my dad might take me golfing or even buy me golf supplies. These people have really affected my life in a good way.

━━━ Student Sample #2: "Two People Who Are Special" ━━━

One special person was my grandpa. He died on June 8, 1998. I have really missed him. He used to do things with me. He was very sweet. He never yelled at me when I did something wrong; he would just pretend it was no big deal! My mom used to drop me off, and my grandpa and my grandma would watch me until my mom got back from going to the mall or doing anything else she had to do which I didn't like. If my grandma was busy, my grandpa would play with me, or they would let me watch television. What I used to call him was "Papa." When my mom picked me up, I told her about the wonderful day I had with my grandparents!

Another special person has been my Grandma Margie. She has been very kind, sweet, and generous. I don't get to see her often, but I have breakfast every once in a while with her. She usually has picked out the place, and it has ended up being really good! I love seeing her. Sometimes she has taken me to the mall and has taken me shopping to buy things she needed. She has also taken me places just to look at some things like the pet stores. She has been sick lately, and my dad and I have seen her more. When I see her, I never want to leave. I have loved her very much!

All About Me *(cont.)*

Teacher Guide

Selection Three: *I See Myself in the Future*

Brainstorm about the future in 10 years, regarding educational needs, demands in the work force, changes in technology, and career choices. For a topic sentence, students may need assistance. As a class, ask students to help write one on the board. Speculation about the future requires future tense verbs. A word bank of future tense verbs relating to career choice would be advantageous in stimulating correct usage and advanced vocabulary choice. Develop this word bank with the class on the chalkboard and have them transfer it to their spiral notebooks. Next, write additional supporting sentences to demonstrate the importance of speculation. Afterward, to address the writing activity, read a student sample below, noting how the writer organizes thoughts sequentially.

Guide the students to speculate about their future in 10 years. Use the student guide outline (page 39) calling for a topic sentence, supporting sentences, and concluding sentences as a model for students to predict their outcome by using their opinions, common knowledge, or any information learned from multiple resources such as family, relatives, books, the Internet, or teachers. The selection needs to be organized chronologically. The importance of a student's choice needs to be written into the conclusion of the selection.

Student Sample #1: "My Future"

There will be many job opportunities ten years from now. One opportunity that would make a strong appeal to me would be to become a ballet dancer. The reason I want to become a ballet dancer is because I love ballet. When I first saw the ballet, I was amazed at their costumes and the way they moved to the music.

I think ballet will make me feel better in the way I act. Ballet will make my legs stronger and encourage healthy eating habits. Ballet could be a workout, and it could make my body look strong and healthy. I love ballet because the dancers move gracefully on the floor. I love ballet because I love to practice, and the dance tells a story.

Student Sample #2: "How Shall My Life Be?"

The age of 21 years will be a new gateway in my life. I will make important decisions, such as which college I will go to, what job I will have, and where I will live.

First, I would like to stay in California for the most part of my life, if possible. But this or any of these ideas will more than likely change. Even with those words, my dream would be to go to U. C. L. A.

Second, my job will influence my life greatly, and I hope to have a wide opportunity to choose. I might be in the field of music, perhaps singing, playing the clarinet or piano, or being a music conductor. Also, I would consider becoming an air traffic controller (ATC), a Los Angeles County Sheriff's Department helicopter pilot, or a private pilot.

All About Me *(cont.)*

Teacher Guide

Selection Four: *Acrostic Poem*

Have students write their first and last names vertically down the left hand side of a piece of paper. Students will then write a short phrase that begins with each letter of their name and is in some way self-descriptive. As an introduction, the teacher may demonstrate an acrostic poem on the board, using his or her own name, letting the students develop the phrases that begin with the letters of the name. Have them complete the poem by using vivid description of their teacher. Encourage them to use descriptive adjectives and verbs. (A student sample for the name "Ryan" is in the student guide on page 40.)

Selection Five: *Bio Poem*

The format of the bio poem needs a detailed explanation. Read and explain the example that follows below, asking the students to follow the copy that appears in their student guide pages. This will help students to understand the structure required. Emphasize that the requirements must be followed exactly to qualify as a bio poem. (Line 6 may be omitted if the student has no middle name.) Remind the students that each line of this poem begins with a capital letter.

Format for the Bio Poem

Line 1—Your first name
Line 2—Three of your character traits
Line 3—"Brother or sister of . . ." (followed by name)
Line 4—"Lover of . . . " (followed by three people, things, or ideas)
Line 5—"Who feels strongly about . . . " (followed by three items)
Line 6—Your middle name
Line 7—"Who needs . . . " (followed by three items you need)
Line 8—"Who gives . . . " (followed by three items you share)
Line 9—"Who fears . . . " (followed by three items you fear)
Line 10—"Who would like to see . . . " (followed by any item, place, or person)
Line 11—"A resident of . . . " (followed by the city in which you live)
Line 12—Your last name

Student Sample

Alison
Artistic, humorous, adventurous
Sister of Erica
Lover of reading, writing, and cats
Who feels strongly about family, music, and friendship
Christine
Who needs knowledge, wisdom, and understanding
Who gives advice, love, and laughter
Who fears heights, sharks, and loss of freedom
Who would like to see France
A resident of Los Angeles
James

All About Me *(cont.)*

Teacher Guide

(handwritten: House of _____)

Selection Six: *Coat of Arms*   *(handwritten: Sketch, approval, colored pencils)*

Students are to design their personal shield or coat of arms and divide it into four quadrants or sections. In each section, students will design and illustrate symbols that follow the format. Students may select which quadrant or section may be used for each selection in their coat of arms. These symbols may be drawn or computer generated. A sample generic shield appears below and may be enlarged, copied, and distributed for each student to use if desired.

An overhead transparency of the outline below may be used to draw examples of appropriate symbols in each section.

A. Something they do well (e.g., art—*crossed paint brush and pencil*)

B. Something important to them (e.g., love—*heart*)

C. Something which represents the past (e.g., child's game—*skateboard, "Barbie"*)

D. Something which represents the future (e.g., career—*stethoscope, computer, bridge*)

(handwritten notes in margin: F / Math / Sports   MG / Draw / Cat OR Bike   D / VB / Sports / Jap Flag   Vet Forensic Scient   college BB coach)

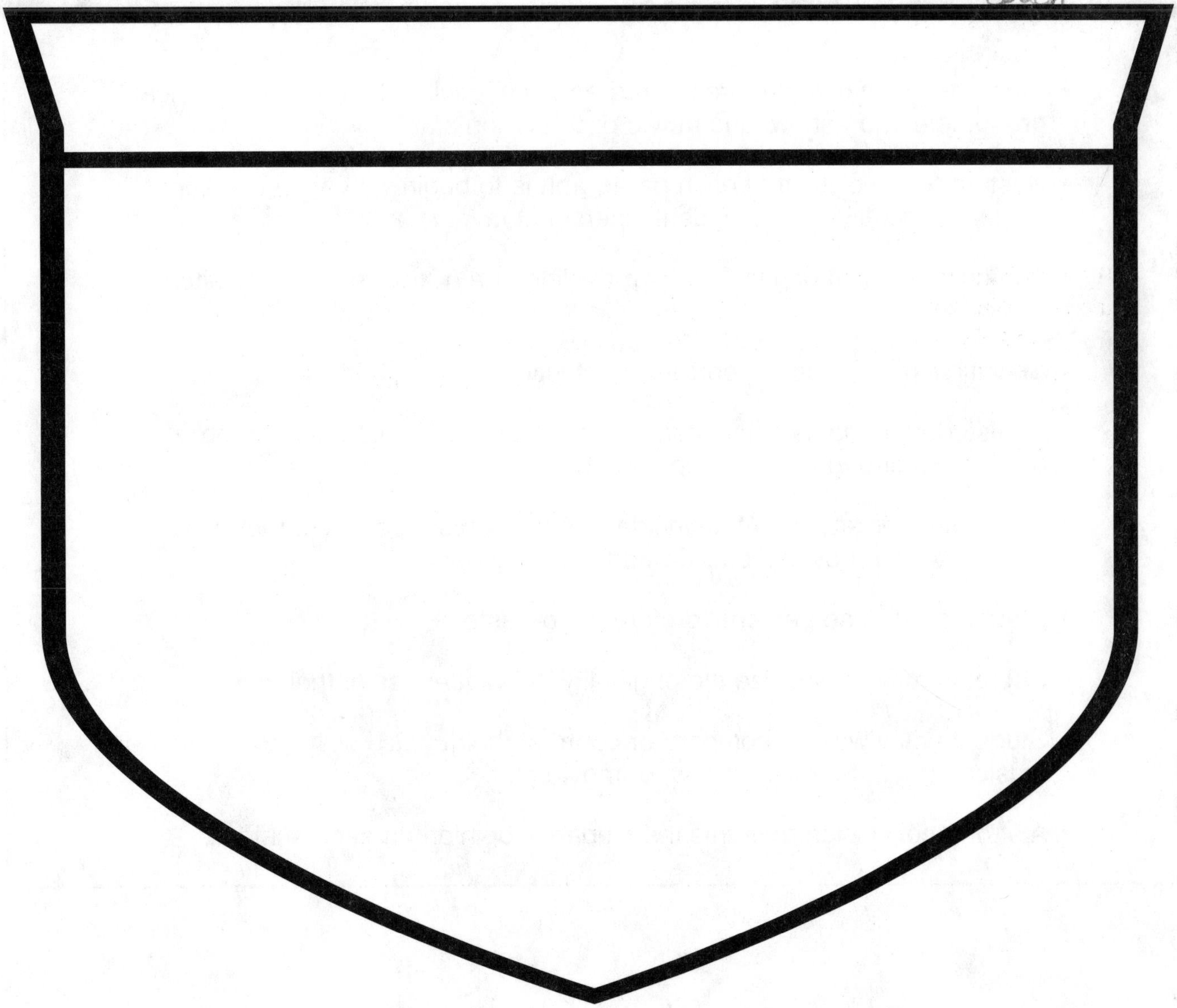

All About Me *(cont.)*

Teacher Guide

Selection Seven: *Personal Favorites*

This selection requires evaluation. Evaluative writing is the most challenging to students, and detailed directed teaching will be required. Begin with class participation by writing a strong topic sentence on the board or overhead projector. Be sure to include the writing prompt. Add supporting sentences that will serve as examples leading to a judgment of why a particular favorite selection was chosen. *Insist on students giving reasons to support their answers.* Since many students have similar interests, have the class brainstorm reasons why choices may have been made. Elicit a supply of reasons from the students, and write them on the board to help the evaluative process. Encourage students to write down several ideas in their spiral notebooks before developing their own outlines. Next, read a student sample aloud (see page 31) to further reinforce the evaluation process in writing. An assignment outline for personal favorites appears in the student guide on page 42.

Points to Emphasize

- Students begin to write three paragraphs describing their favorite musical group, television show, and movie or television star.

- Restate to the class that each paragraph is to begin with a specific topic sentence identifying the student's personal favorite.

- The choices must be justified by providing one or two reasons for each choice.

- Specific examples to support each selection are required.

- The student remains committed to the judgment throughout each paragraph and shows strong feelings about each selection chosen.

- A summary or retelling of an incident or show must be discouraged. A summary only provides background, not judgment.

- Students may use personal preference or taste.

- Students may emphasize the originality or uniqueness of their choices.

- Students may want to compare or contrast their choice with another similar musical group, television show, or movie star.

- A strong conclusion reaffirms the student's opinion on each subject.

All About Me *(cont.)*

Teacher Guide

=== **Student Sample #1: "My Favorite Entertainers"** ===

There are huge numbers of people who entertain me, but three really stand out. First of all, there is Adam Sandler. He is my favorite movie star because his acting is very unique and outrageously funny. My favorite movies he starred in are *The Waterboy* and *Big Daddy*. Adam Sandler is my overall favorite movie star.

Secondly, I'd like to talk about my favorite television show. It's *Malcolm in the Middle* on channel 11 because it is creative, funny, and about boys my own age. Even the parents and the little brother are hilarious. I've liked the show since I turned the TV on about a year ago and started watching it.

Finally, there is my favorite movie. I really like *National Lampoon's Vacation* and all of the sequels, too. The actors and the actresses in every movie do a wonderful job, but my favorite is Chevy Chase. He is very witty and gives amusing facial expressions when he says witty things. I have a variety of favorite movies, but the *National Lampoon's Vacation* movies are my favorite ones of all.

To conclude, I have many people, movies, and television shows that entertain me, but the ones I wrote about are my favorites.

=== **Student Sample #2: "My Favorite Movies"** ===

The three movies I enjoyed most were, *Saving Private Ryan, Backdraft,* and *Air Force One.* The reason why I liked *Saving Private Ryan* was because it touched me to see how those men and women fought for our country. The part that really got to me was when the government had to send a letter to a mother who had lost three sons. It was really sad. The way they had made the movie really interested me. They brought the movie to life. It seemed like it was really happening.

The reason why I liked *Backdraft* was because when I was little (and even now) I wanted to be a fireman. I was interested in the way the firefighters did their job. I liked watching the way they fought fires and saved people's lives. The movie was intense and had plenty of action. It showed reality and what really happened in fires. It gave me more inspiration to want to become a fireman when I get older.

Air Force One was an awesome movie. What interested me most was the way the president's bodyguards protected him. It was also spectacular to see all the weapons carried on Air Force One. I think it was neat that the president had done everything he could to protect his family. I would hope that every person would do the same for their family.

All About Me *(cont.)*

Teacher Guide

Selection Eight: *Remembering*

Students will need to interview an older adult. Encourage the students to interview a close family member who remembers something special or humorous about the student that the student does not particularly recall. Discuss with the students the nature of repetitive stories that seem to come up whenever a family gathering occurs. Remind the class that all family members have precious memories that can be shared. A teacher-shared memory written on the board may bring interest to the class. Model a topic sentence that begins with the identification of the incident that was observed by a family member. Add detailed information that establishes why this incident was clearly remembered by this family member. Present the experience with past tense verbs used throughout the entire selection. Engage the class in establishing a word bank on the board, using past tense verbs that may relate to memories. Have them transfer the words to their spiral notebooks. Next, read a student sample (see below) aloud to demonstrate a memoir. Encourage the students to follow the outline in the student guide (page 43) and make sure their written conclusions reflect the information presented in the body of their memoirs.

═══════ **Student Sample #1: "Pink Rollers Situation"** ═══════

At the age of five, I would sometimes sneak into my grandma's drawer and take her pink rollers. I was not very good at sneaking them out because I would leave a huge mess.

Anyway, I would then take the rollers and pretend that I was a beautician. My grandpa, who would be lying down, would then be awakened when I started working on his hair, which I never did do neatly. I would usually put the rollers in his hair while my grandma was putting them in her hair. My grandma said that we used to fight over them while my mom would just stand there laughing. My grandma also informed me that I would just start mumbling away, like I was really carrying on a conversation while I was working.

It used to be adorable (it still is), but now my grandpa expects it from me at age eleven, and sometimes it gets annoying. What can I say?

═══════ **Student Sample #2: "Remembering"** ═══════

My parents always have told two stories that they think were hilarious, and I guess they were. One time on my first or second Christmas, my dad was videotaping my older brother opening a Christmas present. My dad had set his coffee down on the floor, so I crawled over to my dad's coffee and drank about half a cup of coffee!

The other thing that my parents always have talked about (and I personally have thought it was funnier than the coffee incident) happened when I was two years old. My brother and I were eating yogurt in the kitchen. For no particular reason, I dumped all my yogurt on my head and then looked at my brother. My brother screamed and ran to my mom!

All About Me *(cont.)*

Teacher Guide

Selection Nine: *The Five Best Things About Me*

Each student will describe and define five qualities that he or she feels are admirable. Each quality must be written in a complete sentence with an explanation that states why this quality was a dominant choice. Students state a personal interest that others have recognized as a specific quality. Brainstorm and discuss types of qualities that are assets to people. Students may need ideas such as these:

- Being a caring son, brother, daughter, or sister
- Helping a family member, babysitting, or helping with grandparents
- Doing chores without being reminded
- Being respectful to parents and other family members
- Being respectful to teachers

- Making the right decisions for self-improvement
- Doing well in extra-curricular activities
- Doing well academically
- Being artistic
- Being involved with visual and performing arts

Ask for additional examples of admirable qualities. As a class, develop and write on the board a topic sentence that would show the importance of including all qualities. Read aloud the student sample below to stimulate ideas, to show the writing format required, and to illustrate an example with substance. Have the students use the outline in the student guide (page 44) when they begin writing.

Student Sample: "Five Most Outstanding Qualities"

My five most outstanding qualities are these: being responsible, being athletic, being trustworthy, being a good friend, and being unselfish.

First of all, I am responsible. I am responsible when I tell my mom that I'm going somewhere because I get home at the time I say I will. I am also responsible by doing what my parents tell me. I do everything I have planned, and I don't skip anything.

Secondly, I am athletic. I have participated on ten soccer teams. I show skill in dribbling, scoring, defense, speed, and passing. I have also participated on one swim team. I show skill in speed, freestyle, diving, and backstroke.

Third, I am trustworthy. I am trustworthy by keeping secrets that my friends tell me. I am also trustworthy by doing anything my parents ask me to do.

Next, I am a good friend. I show I am a good friend by helping my friends in their troubles. I also show that I am a good friend by helping my friends stand up to their fears. I help my friends with anything.

Last, I am unselfish. I buy things for my friends and family. I give stuffed animals to my mother to give to kids that go to my mom's hospital. I am unselfish by caring what others want and helping them get it. On Wednesdays, in the morning, I have two kindergartners that I help with letters and sounds. On Tuesdays and Thursdays, I do inventory at my family's store. I encourage and help my brother in soccer, the sport he loves.

Those are my five most outstanding qualities.

All About Me (*cont.*)

Teacher Guide

Selection Ten: *If I Were in Charge of the World*

Read aloud the students' sample poems below and on page 35. Provide the class with copies of the student samples or keep them available on an overhead projector in order to motivate students to write with creativity and humor. Require the students to then write three or more stanzas that would sum up what the world would be like if they were in charge. Remind students that these poetry lines begin with capital letters and include commas. Periods or other punctuation marks are required at the end of each stanza. You may wish to provide copies of the verses below to point out the use of punctuation marks on the student samples.

Student Sample #1: "In Charge"

If I were in charge of the world,
Every sick child would be treated,
There'd be no orphans,
Everyone would be treated fairly.
If I were in charge of the world,
The air wouldn't be polluted,
The freeways would look decent,
Oceans wouldn't be nasty,
Everyone would recycle.
If I were in charge of the world,
Good-tasting food would be healthful,
Everyone will be healthy.
A person who's not perfect,
And isn't always organized,
Can still be in charge of the world.

Student Sample #2: "In Charge"

If I were in charge of the world,
I would help the Middle East peace process,
The ozone layer would not deteriorate as fast,
I would help stop pollution.
If I were in charge of the world,
I'd make ice cream healthful, so you can eat it more often,
I'd make all healthful foods taste perfect,
There could be a cure for everything.
If I were in charge of the world,
I could come up with a plan so everything is free,
And life would still work,
Everyone could have a magical life,
There would be no crime,
Life would be complete.

All About Me (cont.)

Teacher Guide

Selection Ten: If I Were in Charge of the World (cont.)

=== **Student Sample #3: "In Charge"** ===

If I were in charge of the world,
Every day would be Saturday,
You would never have to see a doctor or dentist,
It would always be a holiday.
If I were in charge of the world,
Broccoli would taste like chocolate,
And would still be very healthy for you.
If I were in charge of the world,
School would be like Disneyland,
There would be a skate park on campus,
The drinking fountains would have Coke.

=== **Student Sample #4: "In Charge"** ===

If I were in charge of the world,
All animals could talk,
Brothers and sisters would never be annoying,
Every street would have a skate park.
If I were in charge of the world,
Every block would have an amusement park,
Rides wouldn't have any lines and would be three times longer.
If I were in charge of the world,
You could never get sick,
You could never get hurt,
You could never get bored.

=== **Student Sample #5: "In Charge"** ===

If I were in charge of the world,
Trampolines would bounce twice as high,
You could live on other planets,
There would be no such thing as Pokemon or Digimon.
If I were in charge of the world,
Skateboarding would be on TV more,
The X Games wouldn't come on when you were at school,
School would only be an hour long.
If I were in charge of the world,
Everything would be waxed so you could grind it,
Grocery shopping would be extremely fun,
Parents would always make sense to me.

All About Me *(cont.)*

Student Guide

Check-Off List

Name: _____

Date Due: _____

Materials: spiral notebook, pens, pencils, markers, colored pencils, ruler, construction paper, dictionary, thesaurus, check-off lists, outlines

This writing project must be written in your spiral notebook. This notebook will be used for your rough drafts. All final copies will be done at home.

❑ You may add photographs to your book.

❑ You are required to design an original collage cover.

The collage cover will consist of pictures, words, and symbols cut from magazines, newspapers, bulletins, or advertisements that represent all your hobbies, clothing choices, food choices, music, entertainment, school, friends, and family.

These pictures, words, and symbols will be glued randomly on a cutout profile or other surface to cover the entire outline.

You will need to overlap many pictures and symbols to cover the profile.

After the entire profile has been covered, glue it on the front cover of your All About Me folder.

Write your name under your profile.

❑ You must title each selection with an original title, not the title from the check-off list.

❑ After all the selections have been written, a table of contents will begin as the first page.

❑ Number each page of each selection to correspond with your table of contents.

All About Me *(cont.)*

Student Guide

Selection One: *Childhood Memory*

Write an autobiographical incident about your earliest memory. Describe in detail and in sequence what you remember.

Use this outline to help develop your writing about a childhood memory.

Paragraph I: Topic Sentence: _____

    (Next, provide examples that support your topic sentence.)

    A.

    B.

    C.

Paragraph II: Describe vivid memories.

    A. People:

    B. Events:

Paragraph III: Conclusion *(Tell how important this memory was.)*

    A.

    B.

All About Me *(cont.)*

Student Guide

Selection Two: *An Important Person in My Life*

Write a description about someone important to you. You may write about more than one person. If you choose to write about more than one person, an additional paragraph must be written for each person described.

Use this outline to help develop your description of an important person or persons in your life.

Paragraph I: Topic Sentence

(Describe specific character traits that make this person important to you.)

A.

B.

C.

(Give examples showing why these traits are important.)

A.

B.

C.

Paragraph II: Begin your second paragraph by naming a second person who is important to you.

(Describe additional traits for the second person who is important to you.)

A.

B.

C.

(Give examples that back up the importance of these character traits.)

A.

B.

C.

Paragraph III: Conclusion *(Restate why this person or persons have made such a difference in your life.)*

A.

B.

All About Me *(cont.)*

Student Guide

Selection Three: *I See Myself in the Future*

Write a paragraph that best describes what you will be doing 10 years from now.

Use this outline to expand and develop your writing about how you see yourself in the future.

I. Begin with a topic sentence that shows how you would like to be employed.

_____

A. Describe the education and training that is required for your job.

_____

B. Include a specific job description of what you do at your work.

_____

II. Write about where you would like to be living.

_____

A. Include what difference your job makes in your life.

_____

B. Include what difference your job makes in other's lives.

_____

III. Summarize why you chose this line of work.

_____

All About Me *(cont.)*

Student Guide

Selection Four: *Acrostic Poem—A Letter About Me*

- Write the letters of your first and last name down the left-hand side of a piece of notebook paper.
- Use each letter to begin a short phrase to describe yourself.
- Use descriptive adjectives and action verbs.

Example for the name *Ryan:*   **R**eads suspense books for a hobby

                                          Yearns to be a doctor

                                          Actively participates in basketball, football, and golf

                                          Naturally loves trucks and sports cars

Selection Five: *Bio Poem*

Write a bio poem following the format instructions below and use the student sample as a guide.

Format for the Bio Poem

Line 1—Your first name
Line 2—Three of your character traits
Line 3—"Brother or sister of . . . " (followed by name)
Line 4—"Lover of . . . " (followed by three people, things, or ideas)
Line 5—"Who feels strongly about . . . " (followed by three items)
Line 6—Your middle name
Line 7—"Who needs . . . " (followed by three items you need)
Line 8—"Who gives . . . " (followed by three items you share)
Line 9—"Who fears . . . " (followed by three items you fear)
Line 10—"Who would like to see . . . " (followed by any item, place, or person)
Line 11—"A resident of . . . " (followed by the city in which you live)
Line 12—Your last name

Student Sample

Alison
Artistic, humorous, adventurous
Sister of Erica
Lover of reading, writing, and cats
Who feels strongly about family, music, and friendship
Christine
Who needs knowledge, wisdom, and wit
Who gives advice, love, and laughter
Who fears heights, sharks, and loss of freedom
Who would like to see France
A resident of Los Angeles
James

All About Me *(cont.)*

Student Guide

Selection Six: *Coat of Arms*

Using the shield model below or another that you supply yourself, divide it into quadrants or sections and design your own "coat of arms" that will symbolize you.

You may draw the symbols or use computer graphics.

In each section or quadrant of your coat of arms, try to include several symbols.

Each quadrant or section should display a variety of many of your interests, qualities, and plans.

1. In the first quadrant, illustrate something that you do well.

2. In the second quadrant, illustrate something that is important to you.

3. In the third quadrant, illustrate something which represents the past.

4. In the fourth quadrant, illustrate something which you want to do in the future.

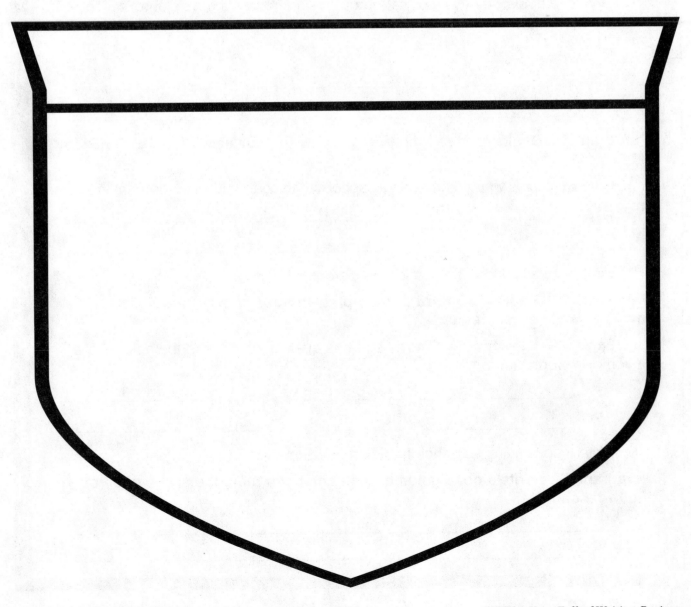

All About Me *(cont.)*

Student Guide

Selection Seven: *Personal Favorites*

A. What is your favorite musical group?

B. What is your favorite television show?

C. What is your favorite movie star or movie?

Write a three- to five-paragraph essay describing your three personal favorites. Each paragraph will contain a different personal favorite.

Use the following outline to help you develop your essay.

Paragraph I: Begin with a topic sentence that will mention your three personal favorites regarding choices in entertainment.

    A. Start your next sentence with your first choice in the music industry.

    B. Give examples why this musical group or singer stands out as an excellent entertainer.

        1. _____

        2. _____

        3. _____

Paragraph II: Begin your second paragraph with your next favorite choice in a television show.

    A. Give examples why you made this specific choice in television entertainment.

        1. _____

        2. _____

    B. Write a concluding sentence for this paragraph.

Paragraph III: Begin your third paragraph with your choice of either a favorite movie or movie star.

    A. Explain why this movie or movie star has qualities that make the actor or the movie worth viewing.

        1. _____

        2. _____

    B. Write a concluding sentence for this paragraph.

Paragraph IV: Write a conclusion that summarizes the importance of all of the three choices.

_____

_____

All About Me *(cont.)*

Student Guide

Selection Eight: *Remembering*

Interview an older adult who remembers something special about you that you do not personally recall. *(Before the interview, write down some questions that you will want to ask. Record the answers and any other details you do not want to forget.)* Try to find an incident that is humorous to share.

Use this outline to develop your essay on "Remembering."

I. **Begin with a topic sentence that includes the specific incident. Mention the older adult who is sharing this past memory with you.**

_____

II. **Give examples or reasons that make this memory stand out with the adult who is being interviewed.**

    A. _____

    B. _____

    C. _____

III. **Conclude with a paragraph telling why the incident was remembered so vividly by the adult but apparently not by you.**

_____

_____

_____

_____

_____

_____

_____

All About Me *(cont.)*

Student Guide

Selection Nine: *The Five Best Things About Me*

Write a paragraph explaining your five most outstanding qualities. Explain and give examples telling why these five qualities were chosen.

Use the following rough-draft guide to help you organize your work.

I. Write down your five most outstanding qualities.

A. _____

B. _____

C. _____

D. _____

E. _____

II. Begin your paragraph with a topic sentence that mentions that you have five outstanding qualities.

A. Explain and give a reason why each quality is outstanding.

1. _____

2. _____

3. _____

4. _____

5. _____

B. **Conclude by telling how your outstanding qualities have influenced the way you are and how they have affected others.**

_____

_____

_____

Selection Ten: *If I Were In Charge of the World*

Write a poem of three stanzas or more that will sum up what the world would be like if only you were in charge. Remember to use poetry stanzas. Each stanza begins with a capital letter and requires standard punctuation.

Holidays with Homonyms
Teacher Guide

Warm-up Activity: Homonym Hunt Game (to be played before the Holidays with Homonyms project on page 47 is assigned)

Objective: Teach students to transfer knowledge of correct homonym usage by using a game format.

Directions:

- Students form into groups of two to four. With a dictionary and thesaurus, students are to find as many sets of homonyms as they can from those sources.
- Allow students approximately 30 minutes to write down as many homonyms as they can find.
- Explain to the students that there will be a competition.
- The teams may be formed by a split down the middle of the room or playing the girls against the boys as a competitive option.
- Encourage the use of homonyms that are uncommon.
- The only team members who will score will be those with homonyms that no other group has written down.
- Use this as a preview for just listing homonyms.
- After one round, students will observe how often all groups wrote down the same homonyms.
- Play the game for the rest of the entire period to notice if there were groups that had written down uncommon homonyms to earn points.
- For homework that evening, have students research more homonyms that would increase their chance of winning.
- Play the game the next day, using the students' additional homonym list. Notice the increase of uncommon homonyms that will add to the competition.
- Keep an accurate tally by which to select the winning team.

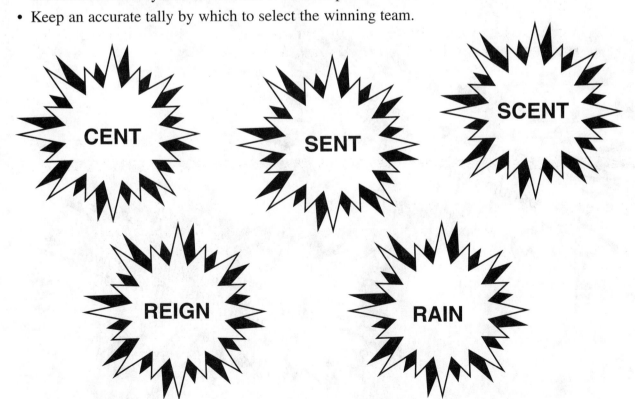

Holidays with Homonyms *(cont.)*

Teacher Guide

Warm-up Activity: Homonym Hot Seat Game *(to be played after the Homonym Hunt and before the Holidays with Homonyms project on page 47 is assigned)*

- After playing the Homonym Hunt, continue with the Homonym Hot Seat Game.
- Students will either pair up or be in groups of three.
- There may be two teams—a divided class, or girls against the boys.
- Each group of students is given a chance to come in front of the class and be in the "hot seat."
- The opposing team will ask the team in the "hot seat" to correctly use a certain set of homonyms. *(If the teacher wishes, the list of common homonyms that appears in the student guide on pages 51 and 52 may be used for additional reinforcement in this game.)*
- The team in the "hot seat" must use all homonyms correctly in a sentence to get a point for that team. There may be a one- or two-minute collaboration before an elected team member says each sentence aloud.
- The opposing team must know the correct answer and tell the teacher if the sentences are correct or incorrect. The teacher will then confirm whether the right or wrong answer has been given.
- A point will be given to each team member who answers with correct homonym usage.
- Alternate each team in this activity until the end of the period.
- A set of homonyms may be asked during the class period only once; no duplicates are allowed.
- Restricting students to using a set of homonyms only once per period keeps them listening, learning, and on task.
- Explain to the students that talking during the game from either team will result in deducting points earned.
- The talking penalty keeps class management and learning at its optimum.

I sent my sister a ten-cent coupon to buy the new perfume with a cinnamon scent.

I'll never forget walking down the aisle of that church on the Isle of Capri.

Holidays with Homonyms *(cont.)*

Teacher Guide

Objective: Teach students to use homonyms correctly in a student-generated, thematically based writing project. (After three days of warm-up homonym games and activities, students should be ready for their writing project.)

Time Frame: two to three weeks

Materials: construction paper, pens, pencils, colored pencils, markers, notebook paper, computer, dictionary, thesaurus

Directions

- Hand out the homonym list from the student guide provided on pages 51 and 52. Students will probably recognize many of the homonyms as ones they have already listed for their own homonym word bank.
- The homonym word bank provided must be reviewed. Students may write quick notes, symbols, or phrases next to each set to reinforce usage.
- Judge the readiness of each class on their knowledge of homonym usage. More review may be needed.

Hand out the student check-off list from the student guide (page 50). Read all the holiday themes and special occasions aloud. Ask students if they can add any more holidays or special occasions. Encourage any additions that may add to the flavor of the book.

Students are asked to write a book using at least 50 total homonyms of their choice. Students may use more than the 50 homonyms required. Since sets vary from two to four words, students may choose which sets they want to include in their holiday book. The student has the option to choose how many homonyms, which homonyms, and what holiday or special occasion to choose. Each set may be split and may be used under different holidays or occasions, as long as the entire set is used. A homonym set used more than one time will get credit for the first use only. Students must be reminded to check off the homonyms that have been used in order to keep track of their list.

The student must identify the homonyms in their writing by using *italics* or **boldface** (if word processing) or by highlighting with pens (if handwriting or typing).

Students may use a combination of computer graphics and/or original artwork to illustrate their work.

The Homonyms with Holidays book must have an original title. A book of 10 pages will be the minimum requirement. On the last page of the book, the student must list the groups of homonyms used.

On the due date, students are eager to share their favorite holiday page. When students read their work aloud, have them both read and spell each homonym to reinforce usage as other students are listening. Illustrate some finished products by using the student samples on pages 48 and 49 to read aloud and or duplicate and display on the overhead projector.

Holidays with Homonyms *(cont.)*

Teacher Guide

=== **Student Sample #1: Presidents' Day** ===

On the last Presidents' Day, we went to Mount Rushmore. We saw a *mail* carrier *go* up to a man, and when he turned around, we instantly recognized this *male*. It was Bill Clinton! I went to him and I *got* his autograph. Another *time* we went to Virginia and saw a picture of President Jefferson (from the *waist* up) in his house at Monticello. That place was kept very clean, and signs said that all trash had *to* be thrown in the *waste* cans. We then went *to our* hotel room, and I read a book on Virginia. We went to a restaurant for dinner that night. It was very crowded, so we walked out an *hour* after *eight* o'clock sharp. We found a McDonald's and *ate* there instead.

=== **Student Sample #2: Halloween** ===

Halloween is just a *night* away, and I am so excited. I will *go* trick-or-treating either as a *colonel* in the Civil War or as a *knight* from the olden times. It might be a little *chilly* outside, but it is going to be okay. After I am done trick or treating, my mom will fix hot *chili* for us to eat. For dessert, I like to eat my candy corn one *kernel* at a time because it lasts longer that way. I see people in many different costumes, which are usually really creative. I always love to light the candles in the Jack-O-Lantern.

=== **Student Sample #3: Valentine's Day** ===

On Valentine's Day just *past*, my family, friends, and I all *met together to pass out* our cards. We all sat in *rows* while a couple people at a time *passed* out the cards. It took us an *hour to pass* out all the cards! My father gave me a chocolate *rose*. Grace, my baby neighbor, then *threw* all her cards into the air right when my mom walked *through* the door with the *meat* for our dinner. Our new neighbors came while we were eating, so we all got up to *meet* them.

=== **Student Sample #4: Summer Vacation** ===

On the last day of school, the *scent* of freedom was in the air and every *hour* seemed like an eternity. *Our* school principal was happy that she had *sent* the sixth graders on *to* the seventh. When the bell rang, the *whole* class, shouting "*bye*," *threw* their backpacks high over the fence. They then crawled *through* a *hole* in the fence, taking a shortcut to the mall to *buy* some snacks.

Holidays with Homonyms *(cont.)*

Teacher Guide

Student Sample #5: Birthday

When I woke up, I saw my parents getting ready for my birthday. We weren't sure *whether* or *not* the *weather* was going to cooperate. I hope I don't get *clothes*, or else I will put them in my *closet* and *close* the door. One of my *present's* ribbons was tied in a *knot*. I finally got it open, and there was a great big TV inside. Oh, how I wished for the *presence* of my brother, who just loves to watch TV golf shows. He likes to *tease* me about my sloppy room, but I get right back at him about all the *tees* he leaves around the house. He *flew* to San Diego to see my grandparents who always get the *flu* when they come here.

Student Sample #6: New Year's Eve

Lots of people have already collected *wood* for their fireplaces. It is a very cold December 31, and in an *hour* it will be a New Year. It *would* be nice to *know* whether it will be good or bad. Our lives could change in the New Year. In New York City, *there's* a big, fat, white ball that makes the official *New* Year's fall. Last year, we *knew* the same things we feel now—that we wish for *no* bad luck, but anything can happen in the New Year. So let's all make a resolution. Our neighbors have made *theirs*. 5,4,3,2,1 . . . Happy New Year!

Student Sample #7: Super Bowl

It's half time, and the crowd cheers for their own team. Maybe now, I think, we can have some *peace*. In the meantime, the half-time show begins. What a *scene*! I've already *seen* a lot of fans showing off their team colors. One even has a banner around his *waist*. How can they *wear* those outfits! *Where* I'm sitting, I look around the stadium and I can *see* a *sea* of people. Many of them *waste* food here, and one even *threw* a *piece* of watermelon onto the field. Suddenly, I see an Air Force jet *plane* *soar* through the sky right above the stadium. It is a bit scary. I can't wait for the rest of the game because my seat is getting *sore* from this hard bench.

Student Sample #8: Halloween

Boo! Halloween is here! Ghosts, goblins, *knights*, and more are out, and I can hear them *groan* through the *night* air. My pumpkin has *grown* very big since I planted it in spring. The people who are trick-or-treating make their *presence* known at our front door. I *see* a witch in the *sea* of costumes walking down the *aisle* to the door. I wonder, *which* one is my friend? Soon, I'll go trick-or-treating, and all my friends will come, *too*. We'll be looking for treats and *presents* at our party afterward. Well, it's time to go . . . Happy Halloween!

Holidays with Homonyms *(cont.)*
Student Guide

Check-Off List

Name: _____

Date Due: _____

Materials: construction paper, pens, pencils, colored pencils, markers, notebook paper, computer, dictionary, thesaurus

Directions: Write a holiday book using homonyms to illustrate correct usage. Focus your book on a specific theme or special occasion for each page. Illustrate each page with an appropriate picture. You may use technology and/or original artwork. Use complete sentences. You may use humor in your book.

- This book must have an original name, a table of contents, and page numbers. The book must have at least 10 illustrated pages.
- You must include at least 50 homonyms total. These homonyms may be used anywhere through the book.
- You may use the homonym more than once; however, you will only get credit for a one-time usage.
- Highlight each homonym used. You may highlight with italics, highlighter pens, or use bold word-processing.
- On your final page, list all the groups of homonyms that were chosen for your book.

Holiday Themes and Special Occasions
(Additional occasions may be added if approved by your teacher.)

- Fourth of July
- Halloween
- Thanksgiving
- Christmas
- Hanukah
- Easter
- Passover
- Memorial Day
- Martin Luther King, Jr., Day
- Cinco de Mayo
- Chinese New Year
- New Year's Eve

- St. Patrick's Day
- Mother's Day
- Father's Day
- Valentine's Day
- April Fool's Day
- Grandparent's Day
- President's Day
- Columbus Day
- Labor Day
- Earth Day
- Veteran's Day
- Election Day
- Weddings

- Births
- Baby Showers
- Super Bowl
- World Series
- World Cup
- Birthdays
- Anniversaries
- Graduations
- Bar Mitzvahs
- Bat Mitzvahs
- NBA Playoffs
- Rose Bowl
- Summer Vacation

List of Common Homonyms

effect	cereal	he'll
affect	serial	heal
		heel
air	Chile	
heir	chili	hear
	chilly	here
aisle		
I'll	chute	heard
Isle	shoot	herd
allowed	cite	hour
aloud	sight	our
	site	
ant		caller
aunt	coarse	collar
	course	
ate		carat
eight	colonel	carrot
	kernel	karat
beat		
beet	council	ceiling
	counsel	sealing
blew		
blue	flea	lessen
	flee	lesson
bolder		
boulder	flew	made
	flu	maid
bridal	flue	
bridle		mail
	flour	male
by	flower	
buy		main
bye	for	mane
	fore	
census	four	maize
senses		maze
	groan	
cell	grown	marry
sell		merry
	hair	
cent	hare	
scent		
sent		

Holidays with Homonyms *(cont.)*

Student Guide

List of Common Homonyms

metal	rain	knows
medal	reign	nose
meddle	rein	
		lead
morning	read	led
mourning	reed	
		sew
naval	real	so
navel	reel	sow
oar	right	tail
or	rite	tale
ore	write	
		teas
pale	road	tease
pail	rode	tees
	rowed	
pair		their
pare	roomer	there
pear	rumor	they're
patience	seas	threw
patients	sees	through
	seize	
peace		vain
piece	stationary	vane
	stationery	vein
pedal		
peddle	steal	wail
	steel	whale
cymbal		
symbol	suite	waist
	sweet	waste
dew		
do	soar	ware
due	sore	wear
		where
find	son	
fined	sun	week
		weak
praise	knight	
prays	night	wood
preys		would
	know	
presence	no	you're
presents		your

Academic Academy Awards

Teacher Guide

Objectives: Teach students to understand the correct use of past tense and past participle forms for irregular verbs in a student-generated writing project. Reinforce the principle that past tense verbs must be used consistently in specific writing selections, avoiding illogical shifts to present tense forms.

Time Frame: two to three weeks

Materials: spiral notebook, pens, pencils, dictionary, thesaurus, a computer

Students will create a book using words drawn from the list of common irregular verbs in the student guide (pages 59-61). This book will be used to develop the correct use of past tense and past participle forms for irregular verbs and will be based on each student using his or her selection of irregular verbs to explain past accomplishments in receiving each Academy Award.

For each identified award, the student will write an account of how the award was achieved and the effect this award may have as a contribution to the entertainment world and to society.

Students may choose a theme of specific movies they have seen. For example, students may choose action/adventure, science fiction, drama, or comedy. Students may also create their own movie titles.

Using an original design to correspond with the award received, the student will create an award for each category. A computer-generated trophy or certificate may be created. Also, a student may draw or create a trophy freehand.

Students should label a separate page in their notebooks for each award. Students will then use their irregular verb groups to find the best choices of irregular verbs to use in describing their efforts, aims, and achievements leading to each award.

Develop a class-written paragraph to demonstrate the expected result. First, select a category of awards and brainstorm an appropriate list of irregular past tense verb forms to write down on the board. Then elicit a topic sentence, supporting details and descriptions to develop and complete the paragraph. Create a strong concluding sentence. Remind the students that no present tense verbs may be used, although other regular past tense and past participle verbs are allowed.

After the completion of the project, the student will choose his or her favorite award and write a "Speculation About Effect" acceptance speech explaining how this particular award contributed to the entertainment industry and to society. This acceptance speech will be performed in front of the class. A master of ceremonies may be appointed, and a mock academy award ceremony may be role-played. Appointed students may hand out trophies or certificates.

Academy Awards

1. Best Picture
2. Best Actor
3. Best Actress
4. Best Supporting Actor
5. Best Supporting Actress
6. Best Screenplay
7. Best Director
8. Best Song

9. Best Costume Design
10. Best Cinematography
11. Best Short Subject Film/Documentary
12. Best Special Effects
13. Best Computer Animation
14. Best Set/Art Director
15. Best Makeup/Hair Style

Academic Academy Awards *(cont.)*

Teacher Guide

Student Samples

═══════════════════ **Best Costume Design** ═══════════════════

I have spent an enormous amount of time sketching the costumes for the movie *Anna and the King*. I was inspired to design the costumes because the producers held a planning meeting. I thought I should buy the costume materials from Asia, and I was paid a tremendous amount of money to do so. I would have given this job to my assistant, but I chose to go myself in order to study the people, their costumes, and their culture firsthand.

═══════════════════ **Best Art Director** ═══════════════════

In *Titanic*, I set my goal early on to recreate the look of the original ship as accurately as possible. I made twelve dives to the real *Titanic* in a mini-submarine built by Russian scientists. The set director rode with me on several trips, and we took thousands of photographs. Out of our hard work grew the amazing detail of the *Titanic's* staterooms, dining hall, hallways, decks, and even her boiler rooms.

═══════════════════ **Best Set Director** ═══════════════════

For my work on *Titanic*, we built an exact replica of the real *Titanic*, at 1/3 scale of the original. First, I chose a very capable group of carpenters, electricians, and welders, who knew their craft perfectly. My lead carpenter made a plan, then I read and approved it, put him to work on it, and I let him handle the details alone. I knew the cost of production could be cut in this way. When the side of the ship burst after it struck the iceberg, our welders blew a large hole in the side of the ship with explosives. The cameraman swam under water to film the water pouring into the ship. He would have frozen, but we gave him a special suit to wear, and we spread a piece of airtight plastic over the camera to protect it. We created our set and then destroyed it!

═══════════════════ **Best Song** ═══════════════════

When I first laid my eyes on the script for *Titanic*, I sat, deeply lost in thought, because I knew the title song of this great movie must be able to perfectly catch the theme of the film. I tore up several attempts until I rose to the occasion and wrote "My Heart Will Go On." When Celine Dion walked into the studio and sang it, I knew we had a hit!

Academic Academy Awards *(cont.)*

Teacher Guide

Student Samples

--- **Best Short Subject Film** ---

For my original short film *Four Dancers*, I was very happy to have received this award. I have known the two elderly couples highlighted in my film since my eighth birthday, July 10, 1997. I first saw Fred and Carmen, and Gene and Ginger at the Manhattan School of Ballroom Dancing. My parents lost the directions to Chuck E. Cheese, and decided to hold a last minute party at the dance school instead. Fred and Carmen shook the dance floor, and Ginger led me to the floor for a birthday dance! I have grown very close to these two couples since then, so it was easy to make a short film about them.

--- **Best Special Effects** ---

I spent a tremendous amount of time working on the special effects for *The Matrix*. First of all, the crew built wire cables to avoid injury to the actors. No cables were ever broken nor had anybody fallen by the end of the picture. From my creativity, the audience was fascinated and left blown away.

--- **Best Computer Animation** ---

For the Computer Generated Images (CGI effects) used in *Jurassic Park*, Phil Tippet and I swung into action. First, we got hold of an old print of the 1950s *Lost World* dinosaur film classic. We froze individual frames of T-Rex, a Triceratops, and a Brontosaurus. We scanned these into the computer and began to make improvements. After we paid a visit to the Museum of Natural History in New York where we studied the bones of a real dinosaur, we caught the action of the dinosaurs running with amazing realism. Phil had led our team of CGI artists to victory again!

--- **Best Foreign Film** ---

I was especially proud that I won this award for my very first foreign film, *Life Is Beautiful*. When I held the completed script in my hands, I thought it was a very good story that spoke directly to the human heart. Immediately, I sprang into action. First, I sent a film crew ahead to Italy, and then I flew over myself. I felt Italy was best because this story had to be told in a country where people actually left their homes to go to Hitler's death camps. We kept the story very light and comical in the first half. The pendulum swung the other way, and the story got very dramatic and sad in the second half. This contrast of tone was what drew the audience into the suffering of the main character and his family.

Academic Academy Awards *(cont.)*

Teacher Guide

Student Samples

═══════════════ **Best Cinematography** ═══════════════

When I worked as Director of Photography (DP) on *Forrest Gump,* my friend Steven Spielberg lent me a huge crane he had used to photograph the large dinosaurs in *Jurassic Park.* We used this crane for the visually stunning opening shot, when the camera followed a feather as it floated high above the town all the way down to the ground, where it finally landed at Tom Hanks' feet. Later, we drove our entire crew to Washington, D.C., where we shot at the mall with multiple cameras to catch the action as Tom Hanks addressed the rally. This scene would have cost more if we had used only one camera.

═══════════════ **Best Screenplay** ═══════════════

I was very happy to have thought of the screenplay for the movie *Twister.* I caught the stream of ideas coming into my head and fit them into one exciting story. To put it up on the screen, I had to find believable characters. As I kept on writing, I was very excited and couldn't stop. When I finally finished with the screenplay, I had worked all day and all night! Perhaps because I enjoyed writing this story so much, the audience also enjoyed watching it on the big screen.

═══════════════ **Best Supporting Actor** ═══════════════

When I landed my first acting role as the son in *Jingle All the Way,* my dream finally came true—that I could play in a film with Arnold Schwarzenegger, my hero. I was also extra excited to find myself working with Sinbad. When Dementor chased me onto the Christmas tree, I would have fallen off, except that I was actually standing on a board. The film of the people in the street far below was matted to the film of me. Also, the board was digitally erased. I thought of how I would have felt in Jamie's situation, and I was able to deliver the touching performance of a boy who learned that Turboman was none other than his own dad!

═══════════════ **Best Actor** ═══════════════

When I was first offered the part of Sean in *Alaska,* I hesitated because I knew it would require all of my skills and talent. In the film, I led my sister and the camera crew deep into the wilderness of Alaska. We came close to death several times. When I fell down the mountain, I could have broken my neck, even though the part where I hit my head on the rock was faked. When our kayak nearly sank under water, I came up gasping for air. Because of the dangers we had risen above, the emotional scene where my sister and I were reunited with our father rang true with the audience. The real hero of the film turned out to be Cubby, the polar bear who saved us!

Academic Academy Awards *(cont.)*

Teacher Guide

Student Samples

━━━━━━━━━━━━━━━━━━ **Best Director** ━━━━━━━━━━━━━━━━━━

I was inspired by my favorite trilogy, *Back to the Future*, to create my new film *Frequency*. Robert Zemeckis would have paid a large amount of money for it, but the writer sold it to me first. I fell in love with the story about a father who talked to his son by ham radio thirty years in the future. We spent a great deal of time in the editing room, inter-cutting the sequences between the past and the present. Who would have thought that developing parallel action would have created such a fast-paced psychological thriller capable of earning me this prestigious award?

━━━━━━━━━━━━━━━━━━ **Best Picture** ━━━━━━━━━━━━━━━━━━

First of all, I'd like to thank God and my parents for winning this most important of all Academy Awards for my film, *Who Framed Roger Rabbit?* Also, I would like to thank my good friend Steven Spielberg, who was our executive producer on this film. I could not have gotten the enormous amount of money we needed nor have kept my head through the technical difficulties we faced, without his graciousness and fatherly wisdom. I personally would have written the script a little differently. I thought the character Eddie drank too much, and this could have hurt children since he was not a good role model. Despite this one flaw, it was a fabulous picture. Thank you for this honor.

━━━━━━━━━━━━━━━━━━ **Best Makeup/Hair Style** ━━━━━━━━━━━━━━━━━━

Working for hours and hours on makeup and hair was very stimulating and astonishing. I cut hair and put makeup on stars of the movie *Miss Congeniality*. I broke a few rules, but all the stars turned out beautiful. The actors sat in chairs for hours or more getting their makeup and hair done. It cost a few hundred dollars for supplies, and it also cost time and energy. The worst time was when the mousse hit the floor, burst open, and spewed everywhere.

Academic Academy Awards *(cont.)*

Student Guide

Check-Off List

Name: _____

Date Due: _____

Materials: spiral notebook, pens, pencils, dictionary, thesaurus, a computer

Directions: You have experienced receiving all the Academic Academy Awards in a once-in-a-lifetime ceremony. No one has ever received all the Academic Academy Awards in one year of filmmaking. The members of the academy have requested a written statement on how your performance was recognized so highly. What talents and what training did you receive to achieve such incredible recognition in every area of the film-making industry?

As a reminder, the Academy is extremely anxious to hear from you. Please have your written statements ready for the awards ceremony. An invitation for your appearance will be arriving shortly.

Since you have such incredible multiple talents, the academy would like you to design a new trophy or new certificate that would clearly show each specific award that will be presented during the Academic Academy Awards Ceremony.

❏ Please publish this in a book.

❏ You may use a specific movie theme throughout your book, such as drama, action/adventure, science fiction, or comedy.

❏ You may also create your own movie titles.

❏ Please title each page with the award you received.

❏ Each page must have its own award statement and a picture of the trophy or certificate that you created.

❏ The academy members expect to use all of your ideas for future award presentations.

Awards Categories

- Best Picture
- Best Actor or Actress
- Best Supporting Actor or Actress
- Best Screenplay
- Best Director
- Best Song
- Best Costume Design
- Best Cinematography

- Best Short Subject Film/Documentary
- Best Special Effects
- Best Computer Animation
- Best Set/Art Director
- Best Makeup/Hair Style
- Best Foreign Film

Academic Academy Awards *(cont.)*

Student Guide

Since you have been recognized for your past work, past tense or past-participle forms of verbs must be used in each of your statements of accomplishment.

- ❏ Following is the list of verbs from which you may choose.
- ❏ There are four groups of verbs.
- ❏ You must use only the list of verbs given.
- ❏ These verbs must be used correctly.
- ❏ You must use 25 verbs or more.
- ❏ The verbs may be used more than once, but you will get credit for using any given verb the first time only.
- ❏ You must use the verbs from all four groups.
- ❏ Highlight each verb used in your book.
- ❏ On your last page, include all the verbs used in your book.

Group #1

Present	Past	Past Participle
bring	brought	(have) brought
build	built	(have) built
buy	bought	(have) bought
catch	caught	(have) caught
feel	felt	(have) felt
find	found	(have) found
get	got	(have) got
hold	held	(have) held
keep	kept	(have) kept
lay	laid	(have) laid
lead	led	(have) led
leave	left	(have) left
lend	lent	(have) lent
lose	lost	(have) lost
pay	paid	(have) paid
sell	sold	(have) sold
send	sent	(have) sent
sit	sat	(have) sat
spend	spent	(have) spent
spin	spun	(have) spun
swing	swung	(have) swung
tell	told	(have) told
think	thought	(have) thought
win	won	(have) won

Academic Academy Awards *(cont.)*

Student Guide

Group #2

These irregular verbs have different forms for the past tense and past participle.

Present	Past	Past Participle
begin	began	(have) begun
blow	blew	(have) blown
break	broke	(have) broken
choose	chose	(have) chosen
come	came	(have) come
do	did	(have) done
draw	drew	(have) drawn
drink	drank	(have) drunk
drive	drove	(have) driven
eat	ate	(have) eaten
fall	fell	(have) fallen
fly	flew	(have) flown
freeze	froze	(have) frozen
give	gave	(have) given
go	went	(have) gone
grow	grew	(have) grown
know	knew	(have) known
lie	lay	(have) lain
ride	rode	(have) ridden
ring	rang	(have) rung
rise	rose	(have) risen

60

Academic Academy Awards *(cont.)*

Student Guide

Group #3

Each of these irregular verbs has a different form for its past tense and past participle.

Present	Past	Past Participle
run	ran	(have) run
see	saw	(have) seen
shake	shook	(have) shaken
sing	sang	(have) sung
sink	sank	(have) sunk
speak	spoke	(have) spoken
steal	stole	(have) stolen
swim	swam	(have) swum
take	took	(have) taken
tear	tore	(have) torn
throw	threw	(have) thrown
wear	wore	(have) worn
write	wrote	(have) written

Group #4

These irregular verbs have the same form for the present, past, and past participle.

Present	Past	Past Participle
burst	burst	(have) burst
cost	cost	(have) cost
cut	cut	(have) cut
hit	hit	(have) hit
hurt	hurt	(have) hurt
let	let	(have) let
put	put	(have) put
read	read	(have) read
set	set	(have) set
spread	spread	(have) spread

*****Reminder:** The preferred past tense of *sneak* is *sneaked*.
The preferred past participle of *sneaked* is also (have) *sneaked*.

Comic Book Project

Teacher Guide

Objectives: Teach students to write a fictional story creating a conflict and resolution, applying sequential writing, using action verbs, descriptive language, and onomatopoeia, in a comic book format with original artwork and/or technology.

Time Frame: two to three weeks

Materials: spiral notebook, colored pencils, ruler, markers, pens, construction paper, computer

Directions: Before the project begins, have students bring in comic books, daily comics, and Sunday comics. Read them aloud. Ask the students why comic books have never lost popularity. Discuss the different kinds of comics written, subject matter, and the purpose of comics. Ask the students if some comic strips or comic books continue with a daily sequence of events with problems and solutions. Cite examples of comics that fill those requirements. Discuss how comic strips can turn into comic books. Explain to the students their assignment will be to create a comic book using imaginary characters that find a solution to a problem. Use this project to encourage the theme of the enjoyment of recreational reading.

- Students choose the dimensions of the size of their pictures. Each page must have at least four to six panels with related captions.

- Explain that each panel size for the comic book picture must be the same for each page.

- Require that onomatopoetic words such as *bang, boom, crash, clang, buzz, whoosh, swish, creak, eek,* etc., be used occasionally.

- Read the student check-off list aloud to clarify all requirements. Writing the comic strips for each page must precede the artwork and graphics. Excessive violence, weapons, and blood are unacceptable. This project is rated for a general audience.

- Student samples of pages containing captions under blank panels (awaiting the art) may be read aloud, projected on overhead transparencies and discussed, or reproduced for the class if desired as examples (pages 63–73). **A number of students may wish to supply creative drawings to illustrate the captions on these pages.**

- Brief student conferences on each student's rough draft should be held to facilitate complete sentence structure, descriptive adjectives, and action verb usage. Peer editing during this project combines reading enjoyment and student affirmation with skill development.

- The final due date provides the students with a day to read each other's creations. This day fills the classroom with recreational reading and a positive climate for further emphasis on writing for entertainment.

Comic Book Project *(cont.)*

Teacher Guide

Student Sample #1: The Battle for Staples Center *(The samples show the captions only.)*

Page 1

In peaceful downtown L.A., the newly built Staples Center was alive with action.	Inside, Kobe Bryant and the Lakers were playing Scottie Pippen and the Trail Blazers. Chick Hearn, the voice of the Lakers, was doing the play by play.
It was the final seconds of the game. The Trail Blazers were up 102 to 100.	With two seconds left, Kobe threw up a prayer from mid-court, it went in, and the Lakers won the game.
The crowd in the Staples Center erupted. They chanted, "Kobe! Kobe!"	Two days later at Staples Center, the Kings played the cross-town rivals, the Mighty Ducks. Bob Miller was announcing the game.

Comic Book Project *(cont.)*

Teacher Guide

Student Sample #1: The Battle for Staples Center

Page 2

The score was tied. The Kings pulled their goalie with one minute left in the game.	Rob Blake passed the puck to Luc Robitaille in the slot. He shot; he scored to win the game!
On the roof of the Staples Center, the Lakers and the Kings met to celebrate their victories.	Meanwhile, across town at the abandoned L.A. Forum, Dennis Rodman was plotting revenge against the L.A. fans.
Rodman was angry because when he was a Laker, the fans booed him.	The coach released him because of his unsportsman-like behavior, and the fans didn't support him anymore.

Comic Book Project *(cont.)*
Teacher Guide

Student Sample #1: The Battle for Staples Center

Page 3

Rodman was born with the mysterious ability to change his appearance. During his playing days, he was able to change his hair color daily.	After he retired, he learned to transform his whole body to disguise his appearance.
One day, Rodman transformed himself into Shaq so that he could easily enter Staples Center and take over.	On the Laker's next game night, Rodman transformed himself into a bench in front of Shaq's locker.
As Shaq was getting ready for the game, the bench pushed him into his locker.	Rodman, disguised as Shaq, took his place out on the floor.

Comic Book Project *(cont.)*

Teacher Guide

Student Sample #1: The Battle for Staples Center

Page 4

After the first quarter, Kobe suspected something was wrong when Shaq made all of his free throws.	He became more suspicious when Shaq kicked a cameraman in the nose.
At that point even Luc, who was at the game, knew something was wrong.	At halftime, Rodman used a remote-control switch hidden in one of his eight rings to turn off all the lights in the arena.
He used a jetpack to fly up on top of the giant scoreboard hanging in the middle of the building.	When he got up there, he changed back into Rodman and turned all of the lights back on.

Comic Book Project *(cont.)*

Teacher Guide

Student Sample #1: The Battle for Staples Center

Page 5

The crowd panicked when they saw the evil look on his face.	"Now I shall take over Staples Center so that no one will play in L.A."
Luc came out of the stands to join Kobe Bryant on the floor. They assured the panicked crowd that they would stop this evil villain.	Kobe, using his elastic arms, tried to punch Rodman, but Rodman dodged.
Luc tried to knock him down with a boomerang hockey stick.	Rodman was knocked off the scoreboard, but turned into a bird as he fell to the floor.

Comic Book Project *(cont.)*
Teacher Guide

Student Sample #1: The Battle for Staples Center

Page 6

As Rodman safely landed, he transformed back into his original self.	Luc and Kobe chased Rodman into the locker room.
Shaq finally burst out of his locker and ran into Rodman, who went flying into the next set of lockers.	Kobe put a basketball net over Rodman's head, and Luc wrapped his body in a hockey net.
The authorities found the unconscious Rodman in the locker room, tied up in nets. But there was no one around to take the credit for capturing him.	Meanwhile, up on the roof of Staples Center, the heroes celebrated their victory.

Comic Book Project *(cont.)*

Teacher Guide

Student Sample #2: The Adventures of Dancer Man

Page 1

There was once a place called "Boogy Night" where there danced a great dancer named "Dancer Man." He knew all kinds of dances and would dance all night.	One night, some robbers led by a jealous dancer named "Boogy Man" came and tried to steal money while Dancer Man was break dancing. Dancer Man saw and kicked them out with his break dancing.
When the cops came, Dancer Man was moon walking all over the place. The cops asked him if he would become a cop, and he said, "yes."	The next day he went to get his badge at the police station and started right away to fight crime with his technique of using dancing moves.

Student Sample #2: The Adventures of Dancer Man

Page 2

One night when Dancer Man was sleeping, he dreamed that he was at Boogy Night. When he woke up, he needed to go dancing again. But suddenly, he realized that he worked seven days a week.

The next day he asked his boss for a day off on Fridays only. His boss said that he would have to earn it by working hard.

So, for the next few weeks, Dancer Man worked hard at capturing bad guys.

Four months later, he still hadn't got a day off. He was getting angry and was going to burst into the chief's office. But when he opened the door . . .

Comic Book Project *(cont.)*
Teacher Guide

Student Sample #2: The Adventures of Dancer Man

Page 3

	When Dancer Man woke up, he was in the hospital. He wanted revenge for the chief's broken leg and arm and for his own broken leg.
The office blew up with a gigantic boom, and Dancer Man went flying!	
When Dancer Man's leg healed, he went to work as fast as he could, looking for the person who planted the bomb and found him.	When Dancer Man got to the police station, he quickly put the crook in jail, and locked him up. His name was Alex Lumber, alias "Boogy Man."

Comic Book Project *(cont.)*
Teacher Guide

Student Sample #2: The Adventures of Dancer Man

Page 4

After a week, Alex Lumber escaped. He left a note that said, "If you want the chief back, leave one million dollars in the mail box across from Boogy Night tomorrow at 12:30 P.M."	Dancer Man quickly collected the money, and dropped it off at the mailbox. When Alex "Boogy Man" Lumber came to pick up the money, the cops caught him and asked him where the chief was. He didn't say anything.
Thirty minutes later, he finally confessed, "The chief is strapped up in bombs inside and is going to blow up in five minutes."	For the last four minutes, Dancer Man and the cops looked as hard as they could for the chief and found him—strapped with a bomb!

Comic Book Project *(cont.)*

Teacher Guide

Student Sample #2: The Adventures of Dancer Man

Page 5

Dancer Man told the chief to go outside and lie on the ground.	With all his might, Dancer Man kicked the bomb, and it went flying into the sky.
Boom! The bomb blew up with a gigantic explosion.	The next day, Dancer Man asked the chief for a day off. The chief said, "You can have Fridays and Saturdays off."

Comic Book Project *(cont.)*

Student Guide

Check-Off List

Name: _____

Date Due: _____

Materials: spiral notebook, colored pencils, ruler, markers, pens, construction paper, and computer

Comic Book Characteristics

1. Comic books are about imaginary, fictional characters.
2. Comic books are meant to entertain the reader.
3. Comic books have a story to tell, which requires a plot.
4. Comic books create a problem or conflict which must be solved.
5. Comic books are filled with action, vivid language, and added humor.

Comic Book Requirements

1. Original artwork and/or computer graphics may be combined.
2. Your comic-book characters must have original names.
3. Your comic book must have an original plot.
4. There is no limit to the number of pages your comic book may be; however, the minimum would be five pages long.
5. If you handwrite, the final copy must be in ink. Use your spiral notebook to write your rough draft. You will avoid losing any pages by keeping all your ideas in your notebook.
6. Each page must have at least four to six pictures with captions included with each picture. You may decide how large each panel should be, but make all panels the same size! Each panel needs at least one or more of the following:
   A. scene or a setting
   B. dialog or script
   C. sound effects
   D. captions or word balloons
7. Your comic book must be in color.
8. Your comic book must have an original cover.
9. Your comic book must be rated for general audience reading!
10. The class will have a "Comic Book Read-Around Day" on the due date to read one another's books.

Comic Book Project *(cont.)*

Student Guide

Use the following outline to expand and develop your comic book.

I. Experiences:

What experiences, real or imaginary, would you like to write about?

A. _____

B. _____

II. Family:

Do you have family members who have entertaining characteristics or traits?

A. _____

B. _____

Could these traits be exaggerated as humorous? How?

A. _____

B. _____

III. Friends:

Do you have specific friends who have extraordinary personalities? Describe briefly.

A. _____

B. _____

Do these friends show humor and imagination in experiencing everyday life? Describe briefly.

A. _____

B. _____

IV. Animals:

Do you have any animals that have shown human characteristics? List those characteristics.

A. _____

B. _____

Do these animals actually pretend to be disguised with a distinct personality? Describe those traits.

A. _____

B. _____

Comic Book Project *(cont.)*

Student Guide

IV. Animals *(cont.)*

Do these animals show a particular sense of reasoning? What would that be?

A. _____

B. _____

Do these animals have a sense of humor? Describe what makes these animals humorous.

A. _____

B. _____

Are these animals trained specifically for a job or mission? Describe that job or mission.

A. _____

B. _____

V. Superheroes:

Could you invent an original superhero with magnificent powers? What are the characteristics of those powers?

A. _____

B. _____

What capabilities would this superhero have that may be original powers that only this superhero possesses?

A. _____

B. _____

Would this superhero save the world from villains, destruction, chemical warfare, or technology hackers? How?

A. _____

B. _____

Would this superhero's purpose be to protect and serve? Explain how he would protect and serve.

A. _____

B. _____

Broadcast News

Teacher Guide

Objectives: Lead students to explore writing broadcast journalism and performing a news broadcast using writing styles for informational and observational reports, problem/solution reports, evaluations, and story. The students will demonstrate the use of creative and critical thinking while using depth, complexity, and novelty in writing.

Time Frame: three to four weeks

Materials: spiral notebook, markers, colored pencils, tagboard, dictionary, thesaurus, computer, Internet access

Directions: This may be an individual or group project that will be written, presented, and handed in by all participants. When a student chooses the individual project, he or she writes all the material and then selects other students to participate in delivering his broadcast news. Therefore, all students are given a chance to participate in additional performances that other students have written. As an individual project, this promotes additional reading of student work and increased visual- and performing-arts experiences. However, it is suggested that students be given the option of choosing either the individual or the group assignment. The benefits of the individual broadcast news are that it encourages additional writing experiences in specific writing styles, thus increasing achievement in reading, writing, speaking, and listening.

✦

As a cooperative learning assignment, students may choose their own groups or be teacher-selected. Groups of three or four work well, but students may want to also work in pairs. Help these groups see that work has been divided equally. Encourage peer proofreading of each article before the project is handed in the day of the presentation.

Before the project is assigned, prepare the students for the demands of broadcast journalism. Ask the class to watch numerous news broadcasts. Discuss the variety of styles that each broadcast journalist presents on television. Ask the students why there are many news channels reporting the same information. Ask students to notice techniques that the broadcast journalists use to keep the audience tuned in. Ask the students what transitional sentences the broadcasters use to keep news flowing smoothly when each separate newscaster begins his segment. Pose questions about how the newscasters keep the audience interested in their program, even during commercial interruptions.

As a first homework assignment, have students watch at least two or three different news channels. Require the students to bring in notes on observations of all channels watched.

✦

The assessment guidelines on this group project are critical to student expectations. Each news broadcast will be assessed as a visual and performance art, as well as a writing project. Assure students that all writing will be handed in after the news broadcast has been performed.

Setting up for the performance is open to student choice. Students may dress in appropriate clothes for their performance. Students may also design microphones or any support material like charts, etc. These performances may be taped as a practice or rehearsal to show students what improvements may be made for their final performance.

Broadcast News (cont.)

Teacher Guide

You may wish to reproduce, distribute, and read aloud (or have students read aloud) the sample script and sample news reports that follow below and on pages 79–88 as demonstrations of previous student products.

Sample #1 is formatted like a play script for three anchors working at one desk. It illustrates an attempt to reproduce some of the chatty, informal banter encouraged rather widely in many contemporary local news channels. Sample #2 presents each separate report as an unbroken monologue to be delivered more formally to the camera. The anchor might deliver all reports, but it is more realistic, of course, if the anchor calls on separate reporters to deliver each presentation. All of these styles may be blended into one news program, thus providing the students with different writing (and performing) experiences.

Student Sample #1: News Script for Who Rocks News—Channel 1

(news script for three anchors: A, R, and N)

A: Hello, and welcome to Who Rocks News—Channel 1.

R & N: We do!

A: What are you doing?

R: You know, you said, "Who rocks?" So we said, "We do!"

A: Okay, whatever! Can we please get to the news now?

N: Go ahead.

A: *(A gives N a strange look.)* First off, I'd like to say happy birthday to the following . . .

N: I . . . We don't have the time for that!

A: Fine! Happy birthday to anyone who has a birthday in February!

R: It's now time for our science report.

A: That's right. A recent study has proved that taller men are more likely to get married and/or have children. But no matter how tall and attractive that man may be, science has also proven that women more than likely would marry a rich and powerful short man.

N: What is the regular height for men?

Student Sample #1: News Script for Who Rocks News—Channel 1 *(cont.)*

A: Well, it says here that 5 foot 6 inches is.

N: Oh, I see now. *(A & N smile and wait for R, who is staring into space.)*

A & N: Mmmmm!

R: Oh, now! Well, it's now time for the weather—local weather, that is. *(R walks over and gets the booklet.)*

R: Well, lately we've been recording highs in the 60s. The sky has been foggy, and humidity has been 89%. We're finally getting out of the 60s and moving into the 70s. Our highs now are around 78-79 degrees. *(R's hand follows the arrows, and R talks at the same time.)*

R: The fog has finally left us locally and is now moving upwards. (R circles the clear area on the map with his or her hand.)

R: Our skies are now beautiful and clear. *(Lets go of the map.)*

R: We're expecting a light rain on Saturday and Sunday. Our humidity is at 51%. As for today, it's expected to be sunny, warm, and a bit chilly in the morning.

N: Yeah, yeah, very nice. Now move! It's my turn!

A: Oh, gosh. *(Refers to the map.)*

N: As for us, we're doing fine in weather, but nationally it's a different story. All through the nation it's a bit cold and foggy. *(Points to the sunnier states.)*

N: Although some of the luckier states have cloudy skies but sunny temperatures, the unlucky ones, like New York, are having cloudy, cold, ugly, mucky temperatures.

N: The nation's skies are very foggy. Their highs are in the 60s, and the lows are in the 50s, with the exception of some of the colder states, like New York, where it is even beginning to get snow! So to those of you trapped in the cold and the snow, take care and keep warm! Back to you, A.

Broadcast News *(cont.)*

Teacher Guide

Student Sample #1: News Script for Who Rocks News—Channel 1 *(cont.)*

A: Wow! That's some weather we're having. But let's just move right into entertainment. N., will you please bring us up to date?

N: First, let's talk about movies—award-winning movies, that is. The votes are in, and the People's Choice Awards went on live, last night. As for Most Dramatic and Greatest Movie, *The Sixth Sense* won . . . right? Wrong! Once the judges recounted the votes, they discovered that *The Sixth Sense* did not win, but *Bicentennial Man* did! Imagine the heartache when that little boy had to give his award to the Pepsi Girl. It was hilarious. He started to cry! Ah, well, that's life!

A: You know, I really enjoyed that movie, *Bicentennial Man*, because it is interesting, sad, humorous, and all around just a great movie.

R: Well, personally, I thought *The Sixth Sense* was a great movie because it's an eye-opening movie that keeps you on the edge of your seat. I'm sorry, but *Bicentennial Man* doesn't.

N: Well, I haven't seen either.

R: Okay, moving on.

A: Oh, before I forget, for the movie review, we give *Bicentennial Man* 4 stars (*with 5 being the highest*), and *The Sixth Sense*, 5 stars.

N: Speaking of this, it is time for fashion!

A: What does fashion have to do with this?

N: Do you want the long version, or do you want the short version?

R: Well, how about the . . .

A: Just go ahead.

N: Thank you. Well, the newest fashion is Weirgly Beads! They come in all designs, and they bring you good luck! Not only that, since the styles are so weird and outrageous, they go with any outfit, and I mean it, too! To find them, just go to any clothes store—for instance, Fashion Q, Mervyn's, or Clothestime. We'll be following up on this story during our commercial break.

Teacher Guide

Student Sample #1: News Script for Who Rocks News—Channel 1 *(cont.)*

A: Aren't you going to do an evaluation?

N: Didn't I just tell you that we'll follow up on them during the commercial? I'll do the evaluation then.

A: Fine! Moving on . . . oh my! This just in . . . *(then A reads a report and ad-libs a bit)* Wow, talk about a low temperature, can you believe that Britney? Anyway, as for music, let's discuss the song "Crazy" by Britney Spears and Britney herself.

R: I think that it is a great song to dance to, but she needs to concentrate on less body and more dancing.

A: That is true, but hey, if she wants to be a Barbie Doll, then it's up to her! About the song, I think it's a great song. If you really listen, there is a great little story in there.

N: I know what you both mean. I truly believe that if she comes out from behind that wall of makeup and plastic, then she could truly be beautiful.

R: Coming up next is Breaking News, Traffic Update, Sports, and the Warm Fuzzy segment. But first, a commercial break; we'll be right back.

(Commercial Break)

X: Hello, I'm Alli, and you need to listen to this: What's ugly but cute and cool and lucky?

X: Weirgly Beads are! They come in wild designs that go with anything and everything! You can make them into a finger bracelet, armband, or necklace. They come in all sizes, or you can have them especially made by calling, 1-800-WEIRGLY *(Never mind the 8th number.)* You can purchase them at any clothes store for at least $5.00. They're guaranteed to be fashionable. Soon everyone will be wearing them.

Y: Like, oh my gosh, I just like, love that! Tyeshia, isn't that just so cool!

Student Sample #1: News Script for Who Rocks News—Channel 1 *(cont.)*

Z: Really, girlfriend, that is just like the bomb-biggity!

X: So, get with the program and get Weirgly Beads!

(Back to the News)

R: Hi! And welcome back!

A: You know what? I love those Weirgly Beads. They're fashionable, cool, and cute. What a great product!

N: How about moving on to sports?

R: Great idea! I'll take care of this one. You've heard of Michael Jordan playing basketball and then baseball. But has this all-star changed his career again? He certainly has! Michael Jordan, the retired Bull's all-time great player, has changed his career again, but this time he changed it to . . . hockey! After a recent interview with Michael, I discovered that he was bored all day at home with his children. He responded to my questions, and I quote, "I love spending time with my kids, but I need to do something," unquote. I asked him why he doesn't return to basketball. He replied that he is sick of it, so he took a new route, hockey. Michael said that he enjoys hockey and hopes to make it a major career.

A: Good luck, Michael, to you and yours. Now, how about our hitting the freeways in our traffic update? Following this, stay with us for our Warm and Fuzzy segment and Breaking News.

R: So, what about those freeways?

A: The 5 Freeway is backed up for miles. To be exact, it's backed up from Katella to Rosecrans. All of this is due to an overturned cement truck. The cement has covered the freeway, and they are expecting the backup to last for over 12 hours! There have been no injuries reported. If this is where you are headed, try taking the 57 to the 91. If you happen to be trapped as of now, then try exiting on Lincoln, and take the side streets to your destination. The 55 is backed up for about eight miles due to a three-car accident involving trucks containing animal carriers.

Broadcast News *(cont.)*

Teacher Guide

Student Sample #1: News Script for Who Rocks News—Channel 1 *(cont.)*

A: *(cont.)* No injuries have been reported, and all animals have escaped safely. Actually, the animals are running around as we speak. To those of you stuck, not to worry, because it should be cleared up in less than an hour. We will keep you posted.

N: Can we go to the Warm and Fuzzy segment now?

A: Yes, go ahead!

N: Hooray! We've heard of D.K.N.Y. and Fubu, but E.B.O.? A group of five single parents (one man and four women) wanted more money, a new career, and a better life for their kids. What do they do with a mind full of ideas and a whole lot of creativity? They start a new business, which they named E.B.O.! They were faced with rejections, disappointments, and very little faith. Numerous companies and businesses told them that they would fail in a week. They were even starting to believe it. They still held on, and you know what? They're making it! The money is rolling in, and they're becoming more popular by the minute. They had faith in themselves, so we have faith in them. We wish them the best of luck and remember . . . Buy E.B.O.!

R: Thank you, N. Now, I'd like you to give a huge round of applause to Detective A.M. Thank you! This is case number 538800. I was walking down the street smelling the delicious smell of chocolate cake, when I suddenly heard a scream . . . AHH! I ran about three houses down when I saw a little old woman spouting tears on her porch. I asked, "What's the matter?" She replied, "My delicious chocolate cake is gone." She explained to me that she had just placed the cake on the windowsill to cool. When she came back from folding the towels, it was gone! The unique thing about this cake is that it was a gift to her son with a $450,000.00 diamond ring in it. While I was searching around the house, I found footsteps with a little bit of cake frosting on the ground. I followed the footsteps into a dumpster in the next county. I found the plate and crumbs belonging to the cake. After that, I discovered more footprints, even some handprints. I then followed them into the next country!

Broadcast News *(cont.)*

Teacher Guide

Student Sample #1: News Script for Who Rocks News—Channel 1 *(cont.)*

R: *(cont.)* There I found a diamond chip with a side of banana peel, and then I knew I was on the right track. About eight hours, three counties, and a country later, I was led into the jungle. Something then hit me on the head. Once I regained consciousness, there was a huge crowd of monkeys around me. One of them had a diamond ring in his mouth. The monkey's name was Hairy. I took him with me back to the old woman's house and explained what happened. The monkey thought that the diamond was candy. He happily returned it. The best part was the old woman adopted the monkey, and they lived happily ever after.

Case Closed

N: Nice story about the monkey!

A: What did you say?

N: Nothing, I swear!

R: Now it's time for your favorite, but not mine—Breaking News!

A: I hate Breaking News. It's so depressing. Oh, let's move into the National News. Did some people just go too far with the whole weather prediction thing? One man in Orlando, Florida, did. He was so worried about the hurricane predictions for his state that he went to his bank and took out his entire life savings, so he could move to a safer place. Not more than 10 minutes later, he was robbed of every last penny. Fortunately, he suffered no major injuries. But now, he doesn't have a dollar to his name.

R: You know, that is really sad . . . but better him than me!

A & N: What?!

#3256 A Year Full of Writing Projects   84   © Teacher Created Materials, Inc.

Student Sample #1: News Script for Who Rocks News—Channel 1 *(cont.)*

R: Just kidding! Now for Worldwide News. This sad story all begins when a young boy, his mother, and stepfather came from Cuba to America by boat for a better life. Halfway there, they realized that the boat was over the capacity, and it began to sink. Fortunately, the boy survived. Unfortunately, the parents didn't. Now his mother's relatives in Miami want him, and his father in Cuba wants him, also. What do they do? They take it to court! After several weeks, it was decided by the court that he should go with his father in Cuba. But his family in Miami won't give up. They're still fighting. The boy's uncle in Miami has temporary custody of the boy as of now. Until everything is in its place, the innocent little boy is caught in the middle. I feel sorry for that little boy.

A: Audience, let's hear a huge cheer for that boy. C'mon, go crazy!

N: As for local news, how far is too far for officers? One little boy can tell you after an awful encounter with an officer. A nine-year-old little boy was riding his bike right in front of his house and fell. An officer on a bicycle rode up and wrote the child a ticket. The reason was the young boy wasn't wearing a helmet. Luckily, a neighbor spotted this and began videotaping it. The youngster suffered minor scrapes and bruises. Sure, he should have been wearing a helmet, but did the officer need to react like that?

A: Last, but certainly not least, we took a vote from the studio audience to see what the most liked period in school really is. The result was no real surprise—You guessed it: Who Rocks News— Channel 1!

A: It is now time to say goodbye. It has been a great morning. I'd like to thank our news crew, my fellow anchors, and our studio audience. Have a great day!

Broadcast News *(cont.)*

Teacher Guide

Student Sample #2: American Broadcast News

National News	● ● ● ● ●

Last week a man was seen in front of the White House holding a gun. He was pointing the gun at the entrance to the White House. He was accusing the president of being responsible for all his financial problems. Fortunately, newly-elected President George W. Bush was not on the premises at the time. Immediately, the national security guards were mobilized to search for the man, and quickly took a suspect into custody. Investigations are still under way, and the identity of the man has not yet been released to the public.

World News	● ● ● ● ●

In South America the people of Brazil are accusing the president of Peru, Manuel Luis, of stealing funds from the Brazilian government, and sending them to a Swiss bank. Manuel Luis then decided to go to war against Brazil to end these accusations. Brazil's President Gabriel Miguel has sent letters apologizing to Luis, in an effort to prevent war between the two countries. However, people are already very upset, and gathered by the thousands in front of the presidential palace of Peru, demanding proof of Luis's innocence. There are rumors that President Luis has plans to escape to Panama. Our reporters are still engaged in the process of completing this investigation. Stay tuned for breaking developments.

Local News	● ● ● ● ●

Disneyland is not the only main attraction in Anaheim. Now there is a new theme park next to Disneyland called, "Disney's California Adventure," which just opened on the eighth of February. Disney spent 1.4 billion dollars to build California Adventure, a luxurious hotel and retail strip filled with restaurants and shops. The park's main attractions are these: "Soarin' over California," where people are lifted forty feet in the air for a hang-gliding sensation, and "California Screamin'," a roller coaster that hits fifty-five miles per hour in about four seconds, rising nearly eleven stories high at one point. It costs $43.00 per person to get inside the park.

Weather Watch	● ● ● ● ●

Good morning folks, let's take a look at this morning's weather. Coastal clouds are bringing heavy moisture into Northern California. Polar easterlies are sweeping harsh winds down to the Hawaiian Islands. Keep your eyes peeled if you're in Denver, Colorado. Tornado watch says there could be a BIG twister working its way east. Photochemical smog is heavy over New York City this morning; it will go down later this afternoon. Key West, Florida, has reached an all-time high of 99 degrees. Los Angeles' high is 80 degrees, low is 74. This week's five-day forecast is sunny on Monday, Tuesday is slightly cloudy, Wednesday is windy and partly cloudy, Thursday will be light drizzles, and Friday will be bright and sunny.

Broadcast News *(cont.)*

Teacher Guide

Student Sample #2: American Broadcast News (cont.)

Warm and Fuzzy	● ●

"A Glass of Warm Milk"

I always remember a real story that my mother told me about her parents or my grandparents when they came to this country from Mexico. My grandfather and grandmother, Roberto and Elena, came to the U. S. in 1953 with five little children. My mother was only a year old at the time. My mom told me they were so poor that they lived in a garage because there was no work for my grandfather. They were so poor that they didn't even have enough milk to feed all the kids.

One morning my grandfather noticed that a milkman would leave bottles of milk across the street at a neighbor's house. One day he was so sad and desperate because his kids were crying with hunger that he took one bottle of milk to feed them. The neighbor saw him and reported him to the police.

When the policeman came, my grandfather told the neighbor that he was sorry and that he would work to pay for the milk, but the neighbor refused to accept this or drop the charges.

I guess the policeman felt sorry for them and paid for the milk instead. My mom said that the policeman was so saddened to see that they didn't have milk that he asked the milkman to bring them milk, and that he would pay for it. This went on for a long time until my grandfather was able to get a job.

My grandfather wanted to repay the officer, but they never found where he lived. My grandparents have never forgotten Officer Bennett or the kind deed that he once did for our family.

Problem/Solution	●

Joe and Rosa Nash have lived in the quiet town of White Tiger Bay for the past 10 years. Lately, they have experienced a serious bug infestation. They have tried many home products, but nothing worked. Finally, they decided to hire an exterminating company called "Bugs R Us." The company told them that they had to leave the house while the exterminating took place.

The couple decided to spend a quiet weekend away from home. When they got back, they were happy because the bugs had gone away, and they paid their bill of $500.00. But the joy only lasted a few days, for soon the bugs were back!

Joe and Rosa called the company again, and they were told that Bugs R Us would send another worker to correct the problem. Once again, Joe and Rosa Nash left their home, and when they returned they found a bill waiting for them, but still there were bugs!

Fed up, they decided to take matters into their own hands. They secretly placed hidden cameras throughout the house and called the company back again. Much to their surprise when they viewed the film, they saw that the workers had been sitting in the living room, watching TV, and eating their snacks! Once they showed this evidence to the company, Bugs R Us had no choice but to pay all the money back. I guess it became a "bug in their ear!"

The lesson to be learned here is to be careful when choosing a company to work in your home. Get references and always double-check the company's reputation before hiring them.

Broadcast News *(cont.)*

Teacher Guide

Student Sample #2: American Broadcast News (cont.)

| **Fashion** | ● ● ● ● ● |

Today in the chic Bonaventure Hotel in downtown Los Angeles, the world-renowned fashion designer Man U. L. revealed his new line of clothing. Cindy Crawford was on hand to model some of the outfits, as were Tyra Banks, Heidi Klum, and Heather Locklear. Vanna White was the announcer for what some critics described as "the greatest act of creation since Genesis." Of special note were Man U.L.'s evening gown made of a burlap bag with a bow and his tortoise shell jogging outfit.

For those with a sense of nostalgia, the designer revealed his bell-bottomed, bell-topped men's smoking suit with a bell-shaped bowler hat. This display is open to the public through Sunday. Tickets are $25.00 at the door.

| **Science** | ● ● ● ● ● |

We finally have come to our top story. Over the past few years, astronomers have spotted signs of ancient coastlines on Mars, the remains of a vast, possibly life-harboring ocean. But those Martian seashores now seem to be an illusion. In 1997 and 1998, the *Mars Global Surveyor* snapped more than 1,000 pictures of this amazing red planet. Malin Space Science Systems' geologists have captured footage containing purported shorelines. The scientists saw no wave-cut cliffs or sediment shaped by waves. Instead, they found boundaries from the *Global Surveyor*, which showed evidence of giant floods. If all of this is true, Mars has more surprises in store.

| **Movie Evaluation** | ● ● ● ● ● |

Dude, Where's My Car? is adventurous and outrageously funny. This movie is filled with laughter and comedy. The plot for this movie is very comical. The rating for this movie is beyond exceptional. If you have not see this movie yet, I recommend that you do.

In favor of this movie, I give it four stars and two thumbs up!

| **Music Evaluation** | ● ● ● ● ● |

It looks like Backstreet is back all right! With their new album, *Black and Blue,* selling tens of millions of copies worldwide since it came out last November, it's clear that the Boys are back in town. There are 12 songs on this new release, and they display a broad variety of styles, moods, and tempos. From their big hit, "Shape of My Heart," which has a driving pop beat, to the much slower, more whimsical "Time," to the fastest-paced number on the album, "The Call," the Boys have shown that their versatility in writing and choosing songs has improved. In fact, it's very possible several more hits will come off this album before the summer arrives. A strong contender would be "The Answer to Our Life," which has a positive message for kids everywhere.

| **Commercial** | ● ● ● ● ● |

When you get home from work, you don't want to waste your time putting ketchup, mayonnaise, and mustard on your burger. Take out a jar of **Mayoketchard**, which includes three favorite condiments in one. This product is made with the very best ketchup, mayonnaise, and mustard for people who like tasty burgers, quick and easy. Before you reach for your ketchup, mayonnaise, and mustard, just pick up your jar of **Mayoketchard**. We guarantee you'll go back for more!

Broadcast News *(cont.)*
Student Guide

Check-Off List

Name: _____

Date Due: _____

Materials: spiral notebook, markers, colored pencils, tagboard, computer and Internet access, thesaurus, dictionary

Requirements

❑ All students are required to write and perform a broadcast news production. All news segments will be written with appropriate language, and only nonviolent news will be reported. The news broadcast will be rated for general audiences only.

❑ This assignment will be an individual or group project that will be written, presented, and handed in.

❑ All participants will share equally in the jobs of writing their news broadcast.

❑ Each student will be graded individually on the writing and the presentation. Copies printed directly from the Internet will not be acceptable. All news must be written in the students' own words.

❑ If this assignment is presented as an individual project, each student will present his or her news broadcast but will also choose members of the class to help present the broadcast. Therefore, each student will present his broadcast news with the help of other students in the class. It follows that any student may be involved in more than one news broadcast.

❑ If this assignment is presented as a group project, students must be sure to divide up the work fairly, giving choice to each member of the group.

❑ Your group may be comprised of two to four persons of your choice.

❑ Your presentation must be a minimum of 10 minutes.

❑ Prepare visuals, such as charts and props needed for your presentation.

❑ Practice your script often to deliver a polished and prepared presentation.

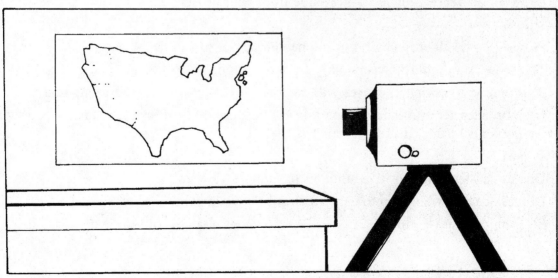

Broadcast News *(cont.)*

Student Guide

All students will be assessed using the following standards and guidelines.

Assessment Rubric for the Broadcast News Writing Process

❑ **Content**
- Ideas are well organized.
- Information is complete.
- All required news segments are completed.

❑ **Conventions**
- Spelling, punctuation, and sentence structure are correct.

❑ **Vocabulary**
- A wide range and variety of vocabulary words provides a newsworthy presentation.

Assessment Rubric for the Broadcast News Presentation and Performance

❑ **Eye Contact**
- Just reading your script may not keep your audience interested in your news.
- Using note cards and periodically glancing at them will increase the effectiveness of the presentation.

❑ **Voice Projection**
- Your voice is loud enough for all the class members to hear.
- Practicing and rehearsing the script will help your audience hear your broadcast.

❑ **Articulation**
- Clearly pronounce each word.
- Do not speak too rapidly, causing your audience to miss out on your important points.
- Practice a consistent pace so your audience is able to understand all your information.

❑ **Content**
- Was your broadcast filled with important information?
- Was your information educational and worth learning about?
- Did your audience gain new knowledge from your broadcast?

❑ **Transitions**
- Provide a smooth presentation from one newscaster to another.
- The broadcast should flow smoothly from one segment to another.
- Appropriate transitional phrases will demonstrate a well-prepared presentation.
- Each broadcaster must know when it his or her turn by the transitions and cues provided by the previous broadcaster.

❑ **Expression**
- Do newscasters with positive attitudes have more viewers?
- Do newscasters who seem to enjoy their jobs have larger audiences?
- Showing a positive attitude and sincere enjoyment of a job well-done demonstrates excellence.

Broadcast News *(cont.)*

Student Guide

First Steps in Preparation for News Broadcast

- Begin listening to the news.
- Notice how the newscasters present their information.
- Notice the different types and styles of news broadcasting.
- Determine what style of news broadcasting fits your personality.
- Notice how each television journalist makes the smooth transition of finishing a presentation and introducing the next segment of the news.

Preparation Outline for Required Segments of the News Broadcast

Use this outline for organizing your broadcast, taking notes, jotting down ideas, and recording specific topics and details to include in your final script.

I. Breaking News

   A. National News (This segment includes all important news occurring in the United States, the most talked about news being broadcast on every channel. This must be factual.)

      1. _____

      2. _____

      3. _____

   B. World News (This segment includes all important news occurring in specific parts of the world outside of the United States. This must be factual.)

      1. _____

      2. _____

      3. _____

   C. Local News (This news includes what needs to be reported from the county or even the city in which you live, whatever is happening in your community that people will want to know. This may be factual or fictional.)

      1. _____

        _____

      2. _____

      3. _____

II. Entertainment

   A. Movies (Evaluate a movie that you have recently seen.)

      1. Describe the type of movie you chose—action/adventure, suspense/thriller, comedy, animation, science fiction—and then describe the theme.

      2. Did you choose that specific movie for specific reasons? Explain why.

      3. Make a judgment on the quality of the movie.

      4. Tell the audience if the movie is worth watching.

Broadcast News *(cont.)*

Student Guide

Preparation Outline for Required Segments of the News Broadcast

II. Entertainment *(cont.)*

    5. Give reasons why the movie is or is not worth watching.

        a. favorite actors or actresses

        b. enjoyment of action and adventure

        c. computer animation

        d. special effects

    6. Give specific recommendations for who should view this movie and why.

  B. Music (Evaluate a CD or music video.)

    1. Explain why the CD or music video was worth buying or worth watching.

    2. Were the lyrics exceptionally written? Why?

    3. Is there a specific stanza that holds special meaning for you? Why?

    4. Does the rhythm of the song make you want to sing and dance while the song is playing? Why?

    5. Qualify your judgment with concrete examples that will back-up your opinion.

        a. _____

        b. _____

  C. Fashion (Review the latest trend in fashion for your age group. You may create your own fashion outfit for both the girls and guys. You may also illustrate the newest in fashion styles from other designers. An entire outfit, which includes shoes, must be illustrated.)

    1. What is the latest style, both for girls and guys?

    2. What are the most popular outfits that girls are wearing to school? You may also include any kind of party, dance, or special occasion dress.

    3. What are the most popular outfits that guys are wearing to school? Guys' outfits may include sports outfits, such as for skateboarders, motocross, and bike competition. Guys also may include outfits for special occasions and dance.

    4. Illustrate your examples. (You may not cut or paste fashion styles out of magazines. You may, however, use magazines and fashion advertisements as resources for your illustrations.)

III. Sports (This segment may be factual or fictional. One or more sporting event may be covered. Any local team that you participate in may be covered in the segment.)

  A. Report the latest sporting event.

  B. Report on any professional sports figures.

  C. Report on any professional sports teams.

  D. Report on college competition.

  E. Report on local high school competition.

Broadcast News *(cont.)*

Student Guide

Preparation Outline for Required Segments of the News Broadcast

IV. Weather (This segment should be factual.)

    A. Local: Give a weather forecast for the week that includes your city. Provide a seven-day forecast, using a visual with your weather prediction.

    B. National: Give a weather forecast for the week that includes major West coast, Midwest, Southern, and East coast temperatures. Using weather-related terms provides authenticity to your forecast.

    C. Explain the current temperatures and forecast any possible weather problems that may occur for the week. Give reasons why weather conditions may change.

V. Human Interest Story (This segment may be fictional, or you may have viewed it on a news broadcast and then rewritten it in your own words.)

    A. Present a "Warm and Fuzzy" story filled with unexpected kindness.

    B. Beginning:

    C. Middle:

    D. "Happy Ending":

Broadcast News *(cont.)*

Student Guide

Preparation Outline for Required Segments of the News Broadcast

VI. Science Report (This segment is factual. Choose at least one of the following topics to be included in your segment. You may add any additional elements that may interest you.)

    A. New Research Information (to be reported on any topic)

        1. What new science breakthrough has been reported?

        2. What facts can you research that relate to science?

        3. What information from the Internet, science journals, science magazines, and newspapers have you researched?

    B. Science Topics (may include any or all of those listed below)

        1. *Technology* (What new technology has been developed?)

        2. *Health Issues on Diet and Nutrition* (What research has been concluded on new guidelines of recommended foods as preventive measures for better health?)

        3. *Medicine* (What kind of gene therapy, new drugs approved by the Food and Drug Administration, or improved or miraculous surgery has recently been performed or made possible?)

        4. *Exercise* (What training and preventative exercise is recommended for living longer, healthier lives?)

        5. *Astronomy* (Have any new stars or planets been discovered? What kinds of telescopes and technical equipment are needed for astronomers to search for additional star formations and planets?)

        6. *Wellness Medicine* (Can prevention of disease through changes and choices in lifestyle through diet and exercise actually happen? What have you found out that may support this research?)

        7. *Inventions* (Have there been any new inventions recently patented?)

Broadcast News *(cont.)*

Student Guide

Preparation Outline for Required Segments of the News Broadcast

VII. Problem/Solution (The story may be fiction or nonfiction, telling how you, as an undercover investigator, discovered and solved a problem for a victim.)

   A. What was the specific problem that accidentally sparked your curiosity?

   B. Who was the victim or victims that were involved with this injustice?

   C. Tell how you found evidence and clues that led you to this important discovery. Write this as a sequence of events.

      1. _____

      2. _____

      3. _____

      4. _____

   D. Write about the steps you took to solve this serious problem.

      1. _____

      2. _____

      3. _____

   E. Conclude by telling how you brought justice and satisfaction to the victim.

   F. Recommendations for further investigations.

   G. Warning(s) to others.

VIII. Traffic Update (This segment may be factual or fictional.)

   A. Provide a local traffic update for daily commuters. Include known freeways in your local area.

   B. Include in your visual the major freeways and interchanges that often get congested.

   C. Provide a freeway map that shows the major freeway system. This map may be drawn, reproduced, or printed from a computer. The map must be large enough so the entire class will be able to see your visual.

IX. Commercial

   A. You must invent a new product.

   B. The product must have an original name and use.

   C. The product may be eaten, worn, or used.

   D. Draw or construct your product for the presentation.

   E. The product may be a combination of products that have been eaten, worn, or used.

   F. You may insert this commercial during your news broadcast at any time. You may create more than one commercial.

Magazine Magic

Teacher Guide

Objectives: Teach students eight writing styles while integrating the multiple intelligences theory into a student-generated project, using differentiated instruction to meet diverse learning styles of all students. Develop skills and increase writing achievement in all language arts content areas.

Integration: This project may be integrated with any core subject taught in the middle school curriculum.

Time Frame: 9–12 weeks

Materials: tagboard, colored pencils, crayons, markers, construction paper, spiral notebook, pens, pencils, rulers, compass, dictionary, thesaurus

- It is suggested that this project be taught in the beginning of February as the final writing project for the class.
- The final project may be scheduled to be turned in close to Open House and/or used for report card conferences.
- These projects display well, demonstrating for parents the writing process, as well as showcasing the students' growth in writing.
- Student skill development is at its optimum, which exemplifies significant student achievement in all language arts content areas.

Portfolio

- This project (the magazine) may be used as a writing portfolio, a compilation of eight writing styles: the short story, the feature article, the advice column, the book evaluation, the interview, the autobiographical incident, the observation article, and the play script.
- This project may also be used as an articulation and assessment tool for the students' future teachers.
- This project reinforces the student's ability to show a product that is reflective of critical and creative thinking using eight writing styles, while addressing content, convention standards, and vocabulary building.

My Magazine

This Month's Contents:

- Original Short Story
- Feature Article
- Advice Column
- Best Seller Book Review
- Celebrity Interview
- Autobiography
- First-Person Report
- New One-Act Play

Magazine Magic *(cont.)*

Teacher Guide

Reminders for Magazine Magic Writing Conferences

Individual student writing conferences are the key to each student's success in the completion of this major writing project.

❏ The teacher schedules writing conferences while the first five activities are being taught.

❏ The writing conferences will be staggered to encourage all students to take time and effort in completing their best work.

❏ Writing conferences are scheduled by the teacher according to the pace of the activities and articles completed by each student.

❏ At the beginning of each class period, ask students which ones need to sign up for a writing conference.

❏ Write the names on the board. As soon as one student leaves the conference area, either at the teacher's desk or a separate conference table, the next student is to come up.

❏ Students are not allowed to stand in line and wait for a conference.

❏ Students are working on the activities assigned while the teacher begins conferences with those who have completed some of the work more quickly.

❏ Begin brief writing conferences with students who may have finished some activities early.

❏ Many of the activities can be skimmed quickly for spelling and convention errors.

❏ The articles will be more time consuming to teach and write. By then, the students will be used to the expectations of the writing conferences.

❏ Students need to be reminded that they must have a writing conference for all rough drafts before a final draft may be written.

❏ The writing conferences may be held for all five activities at once or one at a time. This will depend on each individual student's writing pace and progress.

❏ Rushing students to finish quickly will not produce the quality expected. Due dates may need to be changed, giving students more of a window to produce a top-quality product.

❏ While writing conferences are taking place, students should be working on finishing up one of the activities of proofreading, peer editing, or drawing illustrations.

❏ There may be students who are falling behind. Privately ask the student what he or she needs help finishing. If the student needs help, set up a conference with him or her, offer after-school help, or assign a study buddy.

Magazine Magic *(cont.)*
Teacher Guide

Reminders for Magazine Magic Writing Conferences *(cont.)*

❑ Also, there will be anxious students ready to move forward, for students will be at different stages in the writing process to complete varied assignments.

❑ Staggered writing conferences, therefore, become critical and valuable assets—tools to elevate student's writing performance.

❑ Each day must be used for either directed teaching of each assignment or writing conferences.

❑ The pace and energy in the class are high level; however, the results of the project have direct correlation with facilitating individual needs for student achievement.

❑ The teacher, as the facilitator of this project, must maintain an environment in which students stay focused and organized.

❑ There may be students who have just finished writing the rough draft for the activities but have not yet had a writing conference since they may have needed extra time.

❑ There may be other students who have completed all that has been assigned and may need a conference about all that has been written in their spiral notebook.

❑ The decision to let selected students use a classroom computer or go to the computer lab will depend upon the rough drafts having been proofread by the student and a writing conference with the teacher having been completed. Those students need to bring a floppy disk to class.

❑ There may be instances of a student having rushed through his work; therefore, a rewrite of a specific activity or article may be needed to increase the writing quality.

❑ The fairness of allowing each student equal conference time is important.

❑ Students need assurance and reminders that thinking creatively is time consuming and requires effort.

❑ Share with the students that each person has his or her own learning strengths. Some students can whiz through math, draw anything, jump higher, run faster, or remember important facts. However, remind the class that all students have the ability to use their creative ability.

❑ Tell the students that they all have imagination and they are finding new ways to use it.

❑ Remind students that there may be many solutions to a problem when their imagination is at work and they are using creative thinking.

Magazine Magic *(cont.)*
Teacher Guide

Important Suggestions to Students

❑ Illustrations may be hand drawn, and/or graphics from the computer may be used.

❑ No cut and paste or Xeroxing from other magazines will be acceptable.

❑ By performing periodic notebook checks to make sure that students are staying on task and not getting behind in the assignments, you will help students understand how critical it will be to keep current on each activity and article.

❑ Effort grades may be given with the weekly spiral-notebook checks to encourage students to stay on task to complete each assignment by its due date.

❑ Since this is such a lengthy and time-consuming project, discuss with students the results of procrastination: the lack of quality produced is almost always directly related to poor time management.

❑ The magazine will be worked on every day until it is completed.

❑ Bringing all materials daily to class is essential.

Title of Magazine, Cover Artwork, and Table of Contents

❑ The magazine must have an original title created by the student.

❑ The title must appear on the cover of the magazine in capital letters.

❑ Remind students to put their names on the front cover.

❑ The cover design may include any artwork and/or computer graphics.

❑ The cover may be a clear notebook with the cover design on the front page.

❑ The cover must look appealing, colorful, and thematic.

❑ The cover may use a design similar (but not identical) to that of an authentic commercial magazine.

❑ The table of contents will be the last page to be written in order to coordinate activities, articles, and page numbers.

Teaching the Activities

Emphasize that the check-off list requires only the minimum. Any added articles, activities, or artwork are always encouraged. By judging the pace of the class to see how much time the students need for directed teaching, brain-storming, and writing the rough draft, the teacher will be able to vary student and class completion rates with each activity and article taught. Many students will add extensive detail to each activity assigned, modeling after a published magazine format.

Each activity and article must have an original title, not the title used on the check-off list. Students may organize their magazine activities and articles according to their preference.

The Overhead Projector

An overhead projector, used with copies of the writing guidelines, samples of student work, and clear sheets on which to write, will help students visually understand the directed teaching lesson and its expectations.

Magazine Magic *(cont.)*

Teacher Guide

Activity One: *Vocabulary*

Together as a class, list on the board or overhead projector as many vocabulary words that would relate to a specific theme that has been suggested by a student. Again, pick another theme and list as many vocabulary words the class can think of to relate to this alternate theme. If there are more than a minimum of 15 words listed, remind the class how easy it is to think of more than 15 words that can relate to their magazine theme.

Ask the class what kinds of vocabulary activities would be fun and challenging to do in a magazine. The students should suggest word searches, crossword puzzles, word scrambles, mystery word puzzles/messages, or a variety of other word games they have played that could be written out as magazine activities. Ask the students what would be their favorite vocabulary activity to create that would relate to their magazine theme.

Provide the students with the graph/grid paper for their word searches, and/or crossword puzzles. Word searches and crossword puzzles are the most popular choices. Students almost always use more than 15 words in their vocabulary activity.

Have students staple their rough drafts inside their spiral notebook for safekeeping. Remind the students to provide an answer key for their puzzle activity. This may be placed anywhere in the magazine the student chooses.

Assign a due date for the rough drafts of their vocabulary activity. Write that due date on the board and keep it there until the rough draft has been completed. As a constant reminder to use time management skills, always have the students write down the due date next to any assigned activity. By judging how much time students need in class to write their rough drafts, you may adjust assignments according to students' needs.

In the beginning of this writing project, many students are new to the freedom of student choice and will ask permission often to use their creative ideas. Encourage their choices, reassuring the student that additional creative decision-making can be an asset to the magazine's final product. After the students' comfort levels on creative choices have been reached, requests for permission to choose an alternative or addition to the activity will lessen.

Check their rough drafts on the due date as a follow through. Require that as each activity or article is being taught, students write down the due date for each rough draft. This keeps the students on task and accountable.

Always encourage dictionary and thesaurus use. No spelling errors will be allowed.

Final copies are rewritten at home, which allows for quality individual teaching instruction during class time.

Begin Activity Two immediately after the rough drafts of the vocabulary activities have been quickly checked. Students will be eager to continue.

There may be a few of the students who have not completed their rough drafts on time. A private conference to assess the problem is mandatory. Time management skills, organization, and making the best use of class time can be discussed with those individuals. Suggest to the students who begin to fall behind that they should observe the students staying on task. Allowing the student who needs some assistance to sit near a self-starter may accelerate task completion.

Magazine Magic *(cont.)*
Teacher Guide

Activity Two: *Horoscopes—Speculation About Effects*

Student samples of the 12 astrological signs for models have been provided on pages 102 and 103. Read the student samples aloud to introduce students to ideas about predictions and speculations. Each student writes each sign in his notebook with at least one complete sentence. Students may write more if desired. The horoscope does not have to relate to their magazine, but may. Students are encouraged to bring in samples of horoscopes from current newspapers or magazines as models. Students are required to write only the future tense verbs by using the words "will" and "shall" as helping verbs. As a class, write a few generic horoscopes on the board or overhead projector. Compare the horoscope with a fortune cookie, relating it to future good luck, good fortune, and continued success. Allow *only positive speculations* written by students.

Since fashion magazines tend to include horoscopes as a feature, students who read a variety of these may be familiar with the form. Elicit their help to stimulate class discussion. Of course, many daily newspapers also carry horoscopes, and students may use these as references to model the format.

Some students will want to design an actual astrological sign along with the horoscope, which is encouraged but not required.

When students want to add additional details to any selection of their magazine, point this out to the entire class. To add to all students' resources for ideas, share new examples from other students' ideas. This may help classmates to try additional brainstorming and expand creativity. Keeping the creative climate in the classroom at high levels motivates students to reach higher levels of their potential.

Horoscopes and Signs

Capricorn: December 22–January 20

Aquarius: January 21–February 18

Pisces: February 19–March 20

Aries: March 21–April 19

Taurus: April 20–May 20

Gemini: May 21–June 21

Cancer: June 22–July 22

Leo: July 23–August 22

Virgo: August 23–September 22

Libra: September 23–October 22

Scorpio: October 23–November 21

Sagittarius: November 22–December 21

Magazine Magic *(cont.)*

Teacher Guide

Student Sample #1

Horoscope for May 12, 2004

Capricorn: May will be your month as you discover love and relationships. However, you may also discover heartbreak and hardships.

Aquarius: You will excel in the areas of math and language arts this trimester. Your grades will improve dramatically.

Pisces: In your near future you will find money. You will also be struck with one of Cupid's late arrows.

Aries: Your social life will soar, and if you are popular now, watch your back. If not, you will be.

Taurus: Your life will change for the better in every way possible. Keep your eyes out for romance.

Gemini: Your jewelry collection will grow and become complete. Heartache will come, although others will grow to love and respect you even more.

Cancer: Listen to the questions around you, and you will find a hidden talent. Watch out for love.

Leo: Keep humor and communication going with all relationships that you may have.

Virgo: You will finally take charge of your life and make the right decisions. Others will be proud to follow you.

Libra: Take charge and give your self-esteem a boost. You will also find someone who makes you feel special.

Scorpio: Step out of the spotlight for a while; others will enjoy you more.

Sagittarius: Catch up with old friends; even make some new ones. You'll feel better about yourself.

Magazine Magic *(cont.)*
Teacher Guide

Student Sample #2

 **Aries:** This will be a good month for teamwork, so play a team sport.

 **Libra:** Your finances are good. Buy tickets to see your favorite team.

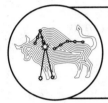 **Taurus:** Avoid physical activity until you feel better. Read *Sports for Kids* instead.

 **Scorpio:** Go bowling this month. You will have good luck.

 **Gemini:** Your teamwork skills are good. To develop self-confidence, try a sport like swimming.

 **Sagittarius:** Do not play baseball this month; after a much-needed rest, you will return to top form!

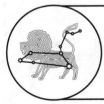 **Leo:** This will be a good month for you athletically, so go for the gold!

 Capricorn: Your teammates will doubt you, but keep going.

 **Cancer:** This will be a good month for you to be a leader.

 Aquarius: Try another position in soccer. You'll like the new experience.

 **Virgo:** Be a spectator this month because your luck is up and you will learn much by watching.

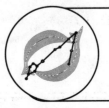 **Pisces:** Soccer is a good sport for you. Play that sport and that sport only!

Magazine Magic *(cont.)*
Teacher Guide

Activity Three: *Jokes, Cartoons, Riddles*

Students may write three jokes, or three riddles, or three cartoons, or a combination of any three. This is only the minimum. Students may write as many as they wish, which more often than not is the case.

The cartoons may be only one scene with a caption or many scenes. Allow the students to choose the style and length of the cartoon. Explain that either style is an effective technique to create humor.

Ask the students why they love reading the comics, and why comics and comic books have lasted over 50 years. Students may volunteer to bring in some comic strips from the newspaper, either the daily comics or Sunday comics, or their personal collection of comic books, and appropriate joke books.

Discuss the different types of jokes and cartoons, and how a variety of cartoons appeal to many different kinds of humor, both from the writer's point of view, as well as the reader's.

Ask the students to name the age group for which the comics are written. Inquire if they know any adults who still read the comics, and share with students that comics are written for adult humor, too.

Ask students why reading cartoons, jokes, and comics for entertainment is so enjoyable. What makes jokes humorous: the subject, the characters, a particular awkward situation, the dialogue, and an exaggeration that is a reminder of a personal experience? Ask the students to think of something humorous in life, something that gives them spontaneous laughter. If students cannot think of an original joke or cartoon, they may pick a favorite joke or cartoon and reword it by changing the subject matter or the characters. Many of the students will try to relate their jokes to their magazine theme. This is not required, but these students enjoy this challenge.

While this activity is being written, students love to share their jokes with one another. Some students will take great time with drawing cartoons, supplying appropriate captions, and showing extensive effort in creating sophisticated humor.

104

Magazine Magic *(cont.)*

Teacher Guide

Activity Four: *Song*

Students will write a song using a familiar tune like, "Row, Row, Row Your Boat," and replace the lyrics with words that relate to the magazine title. Demonstrate how to do this by picking a magazine theme offered from the class and creating a song together, using "Row, Row, Row Your Boat" as the pattern. Write the words on the board as the class suggests them, selecting the best phrasing, rhythms, and meanings as you go. Alternate versions will almost always suggest themselves as the lyrics develop. The overhead projector may be used to model a student sample supplied to help the brainstorming.

Use the exact melody and rhythm of the song while explaining about syllables and beats of a word. In this way, the words will fit exactly into the rhythm of the song. This is not always easy to do, but clapping the beat to different familiar songs will help the class to hear the rhythm.

Have the students think about childhood songs that may be remembered from grade school. "Twinkle, Twinkle, Little Star," for example, has been popular.

Students should write the song first, and then directly underneath the chosen song, rewrite their own lyrics. Encourage at least a four-line song verse with rhyming patterns of ABAB or AABB. Explain that the ABAB pattern means that the first and third lines rhyme, and the second and fourth lines rhyme. The AABB rhyming pattern means that the first two lines rhyme, and then the last two lines rhyme.

Persuade students to write more than one verse. Their song must relate to their magazine and its theme. Ask for volunteers to share their songs when the rough drafts are due.

Student Sample #1 from "Old MacDonald Had a Farm"

Old McSoccer had a team, E-I-E-I-O,
And on that team was Roberto Carlos,
With a kick, kick here, and a kick, kick there,
Here a kick, there a kick, everywhere a kick, kick.
Old McSoccer had a team, E-I-E-I-O.
Old McSoccer had a team, E-I-E-I-O,
And on this team was Taffarel,
With a save, save here, and a save, save there,
Here a save, there a save, everywhere a save, save.
Old McSoccer had a team, E-I-E-I-O.
Old McSoccer had a team, E-I-E-I-O,
And on this team there was Romario,
With a goal, goal here, and a goal, goal there,
Here a goal, there a goal, everywhere a goal, goal.
Old McSoccer had a team, E-I-E-I-O.

Magazine Magic *(cont.)*
Teacher Guide

Activity Four: *Song (cont.)*

Student Sample #2 from "The Itsy Bitsy Spider"

The itsy, bitsy student got up to scream and shout.
Up popped the teacher to bawl the student out.
Down came the principal and cleared up all the noise.
Now the class is happy, all the girls and boys.

Student Sample #3 from "Row, Row, Row Your Boat"

This is a magazine,
All about style,
You will learn a lot from this,
So don't forget to smile.
Fashion's so important,
To everyone today,
Always try to be in style,
It brightens up the day!

Activity Five: *Musical Instrument*

Students will create a musical instrument by drawing it freehand, or they may actually construct it. This instrument must have an original name. On the board or on a clear overhead transparency, brainstorm all the instruments the class can name. Ask students to combine two instruments together and decide what to name it.

For example, combining a violin and a harmonica could result in an instrument called a *viomonica* or *harmoniviol*. Also, combining a guitar with a tambourine might result in an instrument called a *guitambourine*.

 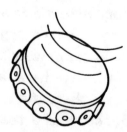

Draw a simple combination of two instruments on the board or overhead projector. Also, ask for a volunteer from the class to draw an instrument. Try naming some silly combinations of instruments, making it an enjoyable activity. Suggest to students that they may also add additional information on the purchase price, availability, and where it can be ordered.

Magazine Magic *(cont.)*
Teacher Guide

Activity Six: *Math Whiz*

Students will create a math activity. Brainstorm together to generate a varied list of math games and puzzles students have always enjoyed and done just for fun. Write down on the board all the suggestions from the class. Allow students to fully explain all math puzzles and games they have done. This generates creativity and builds on students' ideas for their own math game or puzzle.

- Discuss graph art, using multiplication, subtraction, addition, and division. The picture should be an object that relates to the magazine.

- Students may write challenging logic word problems.

- Students may create a spatial jigsaw puzzle that has to be cut out and pasted to find the object created. Students may create a logic game, draw a game board, and write directions on how to play the game.

- Students may create math activities using fractions and decimals in a descriptive story, using pictures of the fractions and decimals to reinforce the spatial elements of the study of fractions.

- Use the student samples supplied below and on page 108 to help students generate additional ideas.

(After the six activities have been taught, some students will finish all activities before the due dates. Additionally, there will be students who may need to be reminded to keep on task to complete all the activities. Remember that writing conferences for all activities need to be completed before beginning the articles.)

Student Sample #1: Math Puzzle

1. Ronaldo's team scored 180 goals, and Ronaldo had a foot on half the goals. At the season's end, he had 42 assists. How many goals did Ronaldo have? _____ (*90 goals*)

2. Wayne Gretzky once scored 92 goals in an 80-game season. How many goals per game did Wayne Gretzky average? _____ (*1.15 goals*)

3. If Mark McGwire hit 70 home runs, 24 doubles, and 64 singles, how many total bases did Mark touch? _____ (*392 total bases*)

4. If Shaq attempted 12 free throws per game during an 82-game season, and he made 50% of his free throws, how many free throws did Shaq make? _____ (*492 free throws*)

Magazine Magic *(cont.)*
Teacher Guide

Activity Six: *Math Whiz (cont.)*

Student Sample #2: Secret Scramble

Change each improper fraction beneath the lines into a mixed number. Change each mixed number beneath the lines into an improper fraction. When you have correctly made these changes, you will be able to decode the secret message.

Key to the Secret Code

A = 7/2	G = 14/9	O = 9 3/7
C = 11/8	I = 25/8	R = 1 4/9
D = 1 5/12	L = 1 2/5	S = 17/3
E = 7 3/4	M = 3 1/4	V = 8 1/3

Coded Message

‾‾‾‾	‾‾‾‾	‾‾‾‾	‾‾‾‾	‾‾‾‾
25/3	3 1/8	17/12	31/4	66/7
‾‾‾‾	‾‾‾‾	‾‾‾‾	‾‾‾‾	‾‾‾‾
1 5/9	3 1/2	13/4	31/4	5 2/3
‾‾‾‾	‾‾‾‾	‾‾‾‾		
3 1/2	13/9	31/4		

‾‾‾‾ ‾‾‾‾ ‾‾‾‾ ‾‾‾‾!
1 3/8   66/7   66/7   7/5

(Decoded Secret Message: *Video games are cool!*)

Student Sample #3: Baseball Math Trivia

1. The number of players on the regular major league roster: _____
2. The number of games played by each team each season: _____
3. The number of home runs hit by George Herman Ruth in 1927: _____
4. The number of World Series won by the Chicago Cubs since 1908: _____
5. The number of times Philadelphia's Mike Schmidt has won the home run title: _____
6. Now add the numbers above _____.
7. Subtract Jackie Robinson's uniform number _____.
8. Finally, multiply by 10 _____.
9. The answer would equal the number of games Lou Gehrig played between 1925 and 1939 _____. (2,130 games)

Magazine Magic (*cont.*)
Teacher Guide

All articles must relate to the theme of the magazine. All articles must be written in complete sentences with the proper usage conventions and correct spelling.

Article One: *The Short Story*

Choose a favorite short story the class has already read aloud. Display the story or the student sample on page 112 on an overhead projector.

Pose these questions:

1. What was the story about? (Lead students to use the terms *plot* and *theme*.)
2. Where and when does the story take place? (Lead students to use the term *setting*.)
3. Ask students to find a descriptive passage in the story.
4. Ask the students to point out examples of the vivid language that has kept the interest of the reader.
5. How does the author get the reader to feel close to the characters in the story?
6. What personality traits, relationships, and personal values do some of the main characters have in the short story?
7. How does the author use dialog as a communication tool? How is dialog written and punctuated?
8. How could the author's writing style be used as a model to help character development, plot, setting, and dialog?

Short Story by Directed Teaching

Using the board or overhead projector to record suggestions, ask the class to brainstorm a short story about a school dance, for example. Begin with a topic sentence, and write it on the board, using the outline (Story Prewriting Guide) on page 110 . Students continue to contribute, writing three or four sentences with supporting details. Next, write a dialog between two characters, using different-colored chalk or markers for quotation marks and punctuation marks. Together, write a conclusion.

Distribute the prewriting guide for a topic sentence with supporting details and the dialog instructions on page 110. Have students staple the instruction sheets into their spiral notebooks. Students will then begin filling out their own story prewriting guides. After completing this guide, students use the notes to write their rough drafts in their spiral notebooks.

This prewriting guide may also be made into an overhead. Some students may need some suggestions for plots that can relate to their themes. Ask for suggestions from other students, keeping the brainstorming dialog alive to stimulate new creativity. Remind students they need at least 10 lines of dialog in their short story.

Students must give the short story a title, capitalizing the beginning word and all others except articles, coordinating conjunctions, and any prepositions shorter than five letters. Write examples on the chalkboard of several famous short-story titles, noting this conventional form for capitalizing titles.

The short story should be at least one handwritten page in length.

Writing the dialog correctly may be a challenging experience in the short-story assignment. Students will need to keep correct dialog examples nearby to help with punctuation and paragraph development.

Magazine Magic *(cont.)*

Teacher Guide

Article One: *The Short Story (cont.)*

Story Prewriting Guide

I. Introduction: Begin with a topic sentence that introduces the story. Develop the setting, the main character who is facing a problem, and supporting characters involved with the problem.

Topic Sentence: _____

Setting: _____

Main Character: _____

Supporting Characters: _____

II. The Body of the Story: Use dialog, action words, and descriptive language.

Create the problem and introduce some suspense with the main character:

_____

_____

_____

Try to solve the problem, using the supporting characters:

_____

_____

_____

III. Conclusion: Conclude with a believable solution to the problem. The solution must be consistent with the sequence of events.

_____

_____

_____

Use this prewriting guide to develop a three- to five-paragraph short story. From the notes developed on this prewriting guide, write the rough draft for your story in your spiral notebook.

Magazine Magic
Teacher Guide

Article One: *The Short Story* (*cont.*)

Helpful Hints for Using Quotation Marks

All types of writing may make use of quotations, but short stories almost always use some dialog—a very effective tool for showing action, plot, characterization, and theme. In fact, some writers develop their short stories almost like plays, with the dialog becoming the main way of telling the story. The basic rules for paragraphing and punctuating dialog are designed to help the reader quickly understand who is speaking and when the dialog begins and ends. The rules and examples below will help you to write your dialog correctly.

◆

I. Each direct quotation "owns" its own paragraph. That means that you should begin a new paragraph every time a different character speaks.

Examples

The group had just finished their meal at the famous restaurant in Bangkok, and they were walking out the door to the crowded streets of the city. Several of them began to talk at once, but suddenly there was a pause, as sometimes happens, and one voice rang out loudly.

"That food tasted too hot and spicy," Ryan complained.

Therese, following close behind him, said, "I loved it! I can never get enough of these hot, spicy smells and tastes."

II. Remember to supply the punctuation mark (usually a comma) before the quotation mark: "P" before "Q," just as it is in the alphabet. Also, remember that only the speaker's exact words are placed within the quotation marks. Indirect quotations tell what a character says but do not try to recreate his exact words. Indirect quotations require no quotation marks.

Examples

1. *Direct quotation:* Ryan said, "That food tasted too hot and spicy."
2. *Direct quotation:* "That food tasted too hot and spicy," Ryan said.
3. *Direct quotation:* "That food tasted too hot and spicy," Ryan said. "I think I may get sick."
4. *Indirect quotation:* Ryan said that the food tasted too hot and spicy and he thought it might make him sick.

Magazine Magic *(cont.)*

Teacher Guide

Article One: *The Short Story* *(cont.)*

Student Sample: "Mystery Shopping Spree"

"Mom, please take me to the toy store to get Nintendo 64!" Jason cried.

"Sorry, Jason, but I'm too busy. I have to clean house because we're having company this weekend. I can take you to the toy store on Friday, but that's the earliest. Why don't you just ride your bike there?"

"It's five miles away, and besides that, I have a flat tire!" screamed Jason.

"Jason Alexander Henderson, one more peep out of you and you'll be grounded for a week! If you'll help, I might even be able to finish cleaning the house tonight and take you to the toy store tomorrow!"

"Thanks, Mom! I love you!"

Jason and his mom had toast and eggs for breakfast. VROOOOOOOOOOOM! The car started up, and they reached the toy store in eight minutes. As they went through the doors of the toy store, bells loudly rang. RIIIIIIIING! Confetti came down in clouds, covering the floor. Employees crowded around Jason and his mother.

"Mom, what did we do? Are we in trouble?"

They heard the loudspeaker say, "You are the lucky 100,000th customer! You have just won a five-minute shopping spree!"

"Mom, I can't believe we've won!"

The store manager shouted, "Ready, go!"

Jason and his mom ran through the store as fast as they could, filling their cart with goodies. Of course, their first stop was the video game section to get a Nintendo 64. In fact, Jason got the last one, along with all of his favorite games. There was a small jewelry shop inside the toy store, to give parents a place to look around while their children looked at the toys.

"Mom, wait here!"

With thirty seconds left, Jason rushed into the jewelry shop and picked out the most beautiful diamond necklace for his mom.

"5, 4, 3, 2, 1. . . BZZZZZZZZZ! Your time is up! Now it's time for a group picture," the store manager announced.

"Everyone say cheese!" the photographer said.

"Cheese!"

After the photograph, the manager congratulated the boy and his mother. As they left the store, they heard people saying good-bye and congratulating them for being the 100,000th shopper.

"Thank you, bye!" Jason and his mother cried.

When they both got in the car, Jason gave his mom the necklace and thanked her.

"Thank you so much, Jason!"

"You're welcome," Jason answered. "This was the best day ever!"

"I agree, son!"

112

Magazine Magic *(cont.)*
Teacher Guide

Article Two: *Feature Article—Report of Information*

Write an article with facts, data, and modern research on a chosen subject. Students must communicate to the reader that this article has recent important and pertinent newsworthy information. Ask the students if they listen to the news on the radio or watch the news with family members. Explain to the students that the article they are about to write will be like news that relates to the theme of their magazine. This article must contain true facts, authentic information that a reader would find fascinating to learn.

Topic Examples

- New safety products designed for sports equipment

- New medicines on the market and information about what preventative or curative purposes for which these medicines are prescribed

- Nutrition guidelines for healthier food choices

- New scientific global research for disease prevention and cure

- Animal vaccines and care

- The latest trend in fashion design

- New cosmetics

- Archeological finds from the United States to worldwide digs

- New car designs with emphasis on safety as well as style

- Motorcycle safety issues and motorcycle designs

- New equipment, accessories, parts, and tools for car or motorcycle enthusiasts

  1. Provide a model by using the overhead projector to show the student sample on page 115 for this article.

  2. Use the prewriting guide on page 114 as an outline form for the feature article. Begin by creating a feature article on the board as an example. Begin with a topic sentence and add supporting details.

  3. Have students begin to write by using the prewriting guide from their notes and then completing the actual rough draft in their notebooks. Require students to write at least one-half page. Many students may want to illustrate the product about which they have written.

  4. Suggest the need to read magazines on their topics, use Internet sources for product knowledge, and bring daily newspapers into class to help them find related topics.

  5. Assign evening reading to encourage the research on the student's magazine theme. This practice should help create students' confidence in thorough investigative writing.

Magazine Magic *(cont.)*

Teacher Guide

Article Two: *Feature Article—Report of Information*

Feature Article—Report of Information Prewriting Guide

I. **Introduction:** Begin the article with the most current data and research on the specific subject chosen.

_____

_____

_____

_____

II. **Body of the Article**

    A. Support the facts with examples and explanations of why this information must be important.

    _____

    _____

    B. Discuss the impact that this new research and data will have on future consumers.

    _____

    _____

    _____

III. **Conclusion:** Summarize your research with recommendations of what others should learn from this article.

_____

_____

_____

_____

Magazine Magic *(cont.)*
Teacher Guide

Article Two: *Feature Article—Report of Information*
Student Sample of Feature Article

"Pokemon—What Is It and Where Is It Going?"

What exactly are Pokemon? Pokemon are all unique creatures that have special abilities, strengths, and weaknesses. Some can cut down bushes while others can fly or teleport out of battle. Certain types of Pokemon can ferry people over water, others can move heavy boulders, and the electric-type Pokemon can even light up entire caves or dungeons.

◆

Pokemon was first released to stores in America on September 28th, 1998. During the first two weeks, 200,000 copies were sold. Pokemon became the fastest selling portable game in American history! After a month, 10,000,000 Pokemon games were sold in Japan.

Pokemon is gaining popularity worldwide with millions of people. Did you know Pokemon is the top-rated cartoon show? It is on television everyday at 7:30 A.M., on UPN 13.

Hasbro manufactures an entire line of Pokemon toys and merchandise. Wizards of the Coast developed a line of trading cards. Even more Pokemon products were made, such as comic books, videos, and much more.

◆

Many are wondering if any new Pokemon video games will soon be released. In June or July, Pokemon Snap will be released for Nintendo 64. Your mission is to help Professor Oak complete his report. He sends you on a safari on the Island Pokemon Preserve to take photographs of all 150 Pokemon. This is a peaceful island, so there will be no catching or battling Pokemon. If it's the battle you want, it is worth waiting for the release of Pokemon Stadium later this year.

If you don't have Nintendo 64, but own a Game Boy, you will be able to purchase Pokemon Pinball this summer. This fascinating game offers a rumble feature to help the game seem more realistic.

One of the most popular Pokemon games in Japan is Pokemon Yellow. Here, the only difference from Pokemon Red and Blue is that you start with Pikachu, and can catch Bulbasaur, Charmander, and Squirtle. This will be available in America sometime soon.

Magazine Magic *(cont.)*

Teacher Guide

Article Three: *The Advice Column*

Students will use a problem-and-solution writing style in an advice-column format, by creating four problems and responding with four appropriate solutions that relate to the magazine theme. Each problem should begin with "Dear _____." The student may use the name of the magazine for the greeting. The closing signature needs to reflect what the problem is about. The problem must be followed with a fitting response.

Ask the class who reads "Dear Abby" or "Ann Landers." Request that the class explain the purpose of an advice column. Explain that they will have a chance to write their own advice columns with both the problems and solutions created by them.

Use student samples below and on pages 117–119 as a guideline and write the first problem together. As a class, write a generic problem, using the friendly letter form to reinforce the format to be followed. More brainstorming may be needed. Try to use both girl's and boy's themes for problems. Require the class to participate in creating a problem and then call on them to generate the solution.

Write the format on the board or overhead and review the rigid rules of capitalization, punctuation, indenting, the greeting, and the closing. Rehearse this a few times with other themes to give students creative ideas of their own. There may be students who will finish the advice column for homework, and writing conferences may need to be scheduled.

Student Sample #1

Dear Raquel,

The problem is that I went to a party and we were all having a good time until all my friends decided to cream someone. I said it would be fine. But what I was really thinking was it would be fine as long as no one creams me. They decided to cream me! When they creamed me, I was so ticked off I didn't even want to see my own face, so I ran into the bathroom, locked myself in, and I cried for two hours straight. I decided to ignore them for the rest of the party. When I got to school, my friends also decided to ignore me. Now I have no friends! What do I do?

Sincerely,
Loner

◆

Dear Loner,

The first thing you have to do is stop being a baby. You have to stop being a baby because if you ever have any other friends, they're probably going to cream you at their parties, too. You don't have to get mad because the worst thing that can happen is that you get shaving cream in your eyes. You can apologize to your friends, and they can accept your apology, or they can forget you. It looks like your friends aren't going to want to be your friends anymore. What you have to do is make new friends.

Sincerely,
Raquel

Magazine Magic *(cont.)*

Teacher Guide

Article Three: *The Advice Column (cont.)*

Student Sample #2

Dear Raquel,

I need help fast! I'm madly in love with one of my guy's best friends. The worst part is that I can't even make eye contact with him or talk to him. What should I do?

Sincerely,
Madly in Love

◆

Dear Madly in Love,

The first thing you have to do is confront him about how you feel. Tell him that you are in love with him. I'm sure that he will understand. Besides, one day the tables will turn, and he will love you.

Sincerely,
Raquel

Student Sample #3

Dear Allie,

I'm 13 years old and in the eighth grade. My best friend has been doing my homework for me since the first grade. Now she is moving to Canada! What do I do?

Sincerely,
Totally Stumped, age 13
Los Angeles, California

◆

Dear Totally Stumped,

It is a pity that your friend is moving to Canada. Anyway, what you should do is try doing your own homework. By paying more attention in class, you'll know what you are doing. Not only will you learn more, but you will also feel better about yourself.

Sincerely,
Allie

Magazine Magic *(cont.)*

Teacher Guide

Article Three: *The Advice Column (cont.)*

Student Sample #4

Dear Allie,

I'm a senior in high school, and it is time for the prom, but there is one problem. I don't have a cent for my prom dress. My family is going through some financial problems, and I am not able to purchase a dress. What do I do?

Sincerely,
Broke, Age 17
Atlanta, Georgia

◆

Dear Broke,

There is a very simple solution. Try having a party, and charge money ahead of time. Hey, that's what Mariah Carey did! (Do not have drugs or alcohol!) Get your friends to help you.

Sincerely,
Allie

Student Sample #5

Dear Video Game Expert,

My mom will not stop playing "Bust A Move." The house is a mess, I don't have any clean clothes, and I haven't eaten in days! What can I do? Please help!

Starving Child

◆

Dear Starving Child,

Try switching the "Bust A Move" label with the "Zelda 64" label while she's asleep. When she gets up in the morning to play "Bust A Move," she'll really be playing "Zelda 64." After about one hour of "Zelda 64," she'll get so bored that she'll never play "Bust A Move" again.

Sincerely,
Video Game Expert

Magazine Magic *(cont.)*

Teacher Guide

Article Three: *The Advice Column (cont.)*

Student Sample #6

Dear *U.S.A. Soccer Magazine*,

I have a very important question to ask. What is the proper way to line up with the soccer ball so I can kick the ball the correct way? I line up straight, but I still can't kick the ball correctly. Please help me out!

Sincerely,
A Person in Need!

◆

Dear Person in Need,

First of all, I thought the question that you asked was excellent and very well thought out. I know exactly how I can help you. You do need some help because kicking is one of the most important things to do in soccer! All you have to do is get your angle right, point your toe down, and keep your knee over the ball. If you're left-footed, take a few steps to the right. If you're right-footed, take a few steps to the left.

Sincerely,
U.S.A. Soccer Magazine

Student Sample #7

Dear U.S.A. Soccer Magazine,

What is the best way to catch the soccer ball, as a goalie, during a penalty shot?

Sincerely,
A Goalie

◆

Dear Goalie,

The best way to catch a ball during a penalty shot is to stand in the middle of the goal, on your toes, your arms up in the air with your fingers spread apart. Be ready to jump or dive in any direction.

Sincerely,
U.S.A. Soccer Magazine

Magazine Magic *(cont.)*
Teacher Guide

Article Four: *Evaluation of a Book*

Evaluation is the highest level of thinking. Evaluation requires a viewpoint, a critique, and a recommendation. Students are required to judge a book and support this judgment with supportive reasons and evidence why the book chosen should be recommended for others to read.

Students with little knowledge of evaluative writing tend to summarize a book. Students should be discouraged from summarizing the book in their evaluations. This article requires strong examples during the directed teaching lesson. It will help to use student samples provided on page 122.

Recommend the following guide to follow in writing an evaluation.

When writing an evaluation, I will want to do one or more of the following:

- Decide
- Choose
- Select
- Report
- Survey

- Dispute
- Verify
- Assess
- Rate
- Grade

- Question
- Judge
- Editorialize

Hand out the evaluation prewriting guide on page 121. Model the prewriting guide work sheet on an overhead projector with a book that may have been read previously as a class. Stress the importance of the writer giving reasons why the book was worthwhile and enjoyable to read. Point out the supporting sentences in the student samples. Explain to the students that these judgments are the student's opinions. Opinions are not wrong, but must be supported with valid reasons. Tell students that they are "literary critics," very important members of a magazine staff.

This article may require more rewrites than others until the student grasps that the aim is not to summarize events but to evaluate the writing. If needed, give students extra time and help to develop reasons to support their evaluation. If a student has never read a book, suggest a book that has been read to him or her or choose a favorite short story that has been read in class to be evaluated. Movie evaluations should be discouraged.

Magazine Magic *(cont.)*

Teacher Guide

Evaluation of a Book: Prewriting Guide

I. Introduction

    A. Identify the book that is being evaluated. Underline (or italicize) all the words in the book title.

    _____

    _____

    B. State a firm judgment of worth of the selection.

    _____

    _____

    C. Give at least three main reasons to support the judgment.

        1. Reason One: _____

        2. Reason Two: _____

        3. Reason Three: _____

II. Body of the Evaluation: Support each reason with examples and evidence. Avoid summarizing the plot or events.

    A. Example One: _____

    B. Example Two: _____

    C. Example Three: _____

III. Conclusion

    A. Summarize and discuss your viewpoint.

    _____

    _____

    _____

    B. Offer recommendations for others to read your chosen selection.

    _____

    _____

    _____

Magazine Magic *(cont.)*

Teacher Guide

Article Four: *Evaluation of a Book (cont.)*

Student Sample #1

Sleepwalker

This heart-throbbing novel was full of excitement and filled with terror. R. L. Stine did a marvelous job of describing this tale in a matter of about 281 pages. I loved this book because of the heart-stopping matter of pure terror in this story. I absolutely love reading terrifying horror stories about people. Hand me a creepy story, and I could sit for hours reading.

I'd recommend this book to kids eight and over because it was creepy. Although there was some inappropriate language used, I give this book two thumbs up!

Student Sample #2

Space Jam

Space Jam was a terrific book. On a scale of 1–10, with 10 being best, I give it a 10. I liked the book for many reasons. One thing I really liked about *Space Jam* was that it was about basketball. I enjoy anything that has to do with basketball. It also had great fictional characters. The characters were cool because they were little aliens, and I liked that. There were also real characters like Michael Jordan and Larry Bird. I enjoyed reading about them.

The plot was also very interesting. It was very funny, and I found myself laughing while I read the book. I give this book five stars. If you want to read a funny book, and if you like to use your imagination, then I recommend *Space Jam*.

Student Sample #3

Chicken Soup for the Teenage Soul

This is a book written by teens and includes topics like suicide, dying young, and drunk driving. It is a series of poems, cartoons, and stories that teenagers can really relate to. *Chicken Soup for the Teenage Soul* also contains important lessons on the nature of friendship and love, the value of respect for yourself, and the importance of believing in the future.

This great book showed me I'm not the only one with problems, and that there are solutions written by teens, not adults. Each story teaches you something in a different way. It is very much like having your own advice column to answer only your problems.

"Practical Application" is one of the best poems in the book. Everyone should read it!

Magazine Magic *(cont.)*
Teacher Guide

Article Five: *The Interview*

Students are to choose an important person who shares the same interests as those covered in the magazine. Ten interview questions with ten corresponding answers to respond accurately to each question are then to be written. Each question and answer must be written in complete sentences.

The class can begin by suggesting a list of important people they could interview who have the same interests as their magazine themes. Try to cover as many magazine themes as the students have chosen, with suggested interview questions and answers. Using the overhead projector or the chalkboard, write down some questions and answers that students have shared.

Students will ask if they really have to interview that famous person. Respond that the students will write all the questions and create the appropriate answers they think or speculate that this famous person might reply with. Thus, the assignment requires that the writers place themselves in the position of the person being interviewed so that they may come up with a realistic and complete response.

The following questions are guides to help the student frame an important interview question and avoid asking needless interview questions:

- **What does the reader want to know that is fascinating and worthwhile writing about?**
- **Does the reader already know that this person enjoys a certain sport or activity? If the answer is "Yes," this question does not need to be asked.**

Students may ask if they may interview a friend or relative who participates in this activity. Respond that a friend or relative would be an excellent source of information for an interview, or they may interview more than one person. Encourage as much volunteer writing as students wish to do. Explain that each interview question must be well thought out, written in complete sentences, and require more than a simple yes or no answer. If the question must be responded to with a yes or no answer, additional information must be added to complete the response. No quotation marks are needed.

Use a simple question-and-answer format as the interview guideline. The students should use their spiral notebooks, using Q & A to introduce interviewer and interviewee in their rough drafts.

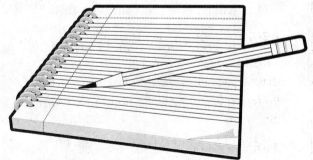

Student samples appear on pages 124 and 125. They may be reproduced and distributed as models or put on transparencies and shown on an overhead projector.

Magazine Magic *(cont.)*
Teacher Guide

Article Five: *The Interview (cont.)*

Student Sample #1

Interview with Christina Aguilera

Q: *How is it, knowing that you are a role model for many young girls out there?*

A: It's great. I love the feeling of being a role model.

Q: *You were able to work with Keri Russell, Britney Spears, and J.C. on the Mickey Mouse Club. Was that amazing?*

A: Yes, I totally connected with them. There was a great vibe on the show.

Q: *What are the best things about touring?*

A: The fans are incredible! They inspire me so much.

Q: *When did you realize you were destined to be a singer?*

A: It was my grandmother who said that I was something more than just a kid singing in the tub. Soon, I was known around the Pittsburgh area as "The little girl with the big voice."

Q: *What are the bad things about touring?*

A: It gets lonely. I don't get to see my friends and family much.

Q: *Are you working on a new album?*

A: I am presently working on three. I am planning on doing a Latin album this spring, a Christmas album for the 2002 holidays, and I am also writing lyrics for my next pop album.

Q: *What do you do in your spare time?*

A: Music is always running through my mind, so I am constantly creating and writing lyrics. But when it comes down to it, I am a 19-year-old girl. I think about boys. I like to go to movies, and I love shopping.

Q: *Do you remember your first kiss?*

A: It was during a game of "Truth or Dare" at a friend's house.

Q: *Did you have fun hosting TRL?*

A: Absolutely! I've always watched the show and taking Carson's job was cool!

Q: *Are any of the rumors about Carson true?*

A: There are so many rumors. People talk no matter what. I try not to let it get me down or bother me. Rumors are just that—rumors.

Magazine Magic *(cont.)*

Teacher Guide

Article Five: *The Interview* *(cont.)*

Student Sample #2

Interview with Kenny Lofton

Q: *Some people will testify that you're the premier center fielder in baseball today. That puts you with the likes of Ken Griffey Jr., Moises Alou, and Bernie Williams. How does this make you feel?*

A: Wow! I mean it's an honor to be mentioned in the same breath with those guys (*laughing*), especially Griffey.

Q: *You had a great rookie year. You broke the rookie record for stolen bases with 66. What non-veteran player do you think has the most potential?*

A: I don't know. My top five would probably be Nomar Garciaparra, Scott Rolen, A-Rod (*Alex Rodriguez*), Vladimir Guerrero, and Derek Jeter. That's not in any order, though.

Q: *What was it like, seeing your face on the front of a baseball card for the first time?*

A: It was exciting. You always dream of it happening and then, WOW!

Q: *You used to play basketball in college for the Arizona Wildcats. Do you think that you could go back to basketball and make it to the NBA?*

A: No, probably not. You have to be really talented to play there now. I just play for fun.

Q: *What was it like to come back to Cleveland after a year in Atlanta?*

A: It was great. I was treated like a king, and the fans are so great. I also liked it in my season with Atlanta. At the All-Star Game in Cleveland when the fans gave me a standing O, it was overwhelming.

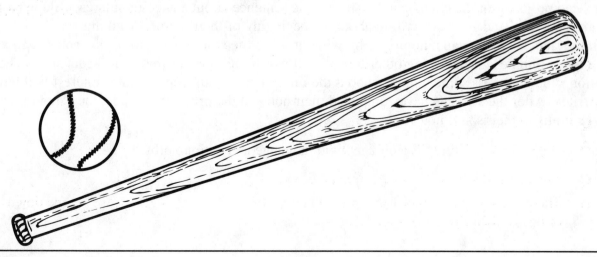

Magazine Magic *(cont.)*

Teacher Guide

Article Six: *Autobiographical Incident*

Students are required to write about a personal experience that is significant and memorable. Often this will explain how they became involved with an interest, hobby, or subject. Included in this, they are to describe a scene which will include remembered feelings, reflections, and relationships. Students will specifically explain about the chosen events that have led up to the significance of their magazine choice.

Have students define autobiography. Students will usually want to volunteer openly and share events in their lives that led up to their magazine choice. Encourage them to share information about their hobbies. Include all discussion, which should generate many student ideas.

Using the brief student sample provided on page 128 (Notice the challenge section following the sample) or an autobiography that has been read by the class, read aloud and discuss why this particular autobiography was written.

Ask students to identify the key elements of their autobiographies that should be included in their writing.

Sample Key Autobiographical Elements

- Remembering childhood events
- Being taught by someone
- Learning something by doing
- Learning something by reading about it and following the directions
- Participating in a competition
- Being involved in family tradition
- Learning at school and desiring to excel
- Participating in a popular activity or trend that many students enjoy

---

Hand out the autobiographical incident prewriting guide on page 127 as an outline for students. Using the overhead projector or the chalkboard, write a topic sentence about a specific interest. Show how to use sequence as the students start writing about the beginning of their theme. Walk the students through the steps of writing an autobiography without using the word "then" to begin each sentence. (Devote a few minutes to suggesting other transitional words and phrases that show sequence.) The conclusion should express some thoughts about the future impact this hobby and/or interest will have on the writer. After the students have completed their notes in the prewriting guide, they should write the rough drafts in their spiral notebooks.

Continue to model proofreading. Encourage vivid language and action verbs.

Magazine Magic *(cont.)*

Teacher Guide

Autobiographical Incident Prewriting Guide

I. Introduction

A. Begin with a topic sentence that gives personal background experience.

_____

B. Give examples that support the topic sentence.

   1. Example One: _____

   2. Example Two: _____

C. These examples can be developed with a paragraph for each—for example:
Personal experiences—How did you personally choose this topic?

_____

Family influences—Did family members influence your choice?

_____

Friends—Do you participate with your friends?

_____

Hobby—Will this activity or hobby continue into a more serious interest?

_____

II. The Body of the Autobiographical Incident: Describe vivid memories of feelings and reflections that stand out.

A. People: _____

B. Events: _____

C. Dialogue: _____

III. Conclusion: Write how importantly the incident affected your life.

_____

_____

Expand this outline into why you chose this magazine theme, and write your rough draft in your spiral notebook.

Magazine Magic *(cont.)*

Teacher Guide

Article Six: *Autobiographical Incident (cont.)*

Student Sample: "How I Became Me"

Sometimes as I walk down the street or while I'm shopping at the local supermarket, I may get one or two people (most likely in need of a job) who ask me how I made *Baseball Magazine*. They usually go on to tell me how their horrible last boss fired them, and explain that they're really such good writers. But getting back to the original question, this is what I tell them.

"I've grown up in a family that loves baseball. I live, eat, and breathe baseball."

I also like to write. Using the words of probably every father (but especially mine), I say, "Always find a job you like to do. If you don't like a particular subject, don't try to get a job that requires the thing you dislike. Don't take that job."

I decided to have a job that combined my love for writing and my love for baseball. The result is *Baseball Magazine*. *Baseball Magazine* is now on its 146th issue and has turned out to be quite a success. In fact, it was named the best sports-related magazine last year. *Baseball Magazine* has a flame, and I hope it keeps burning brightly.

Challenge

A. In the space below, see if you can note how many of the required elements of the prewriting guide are included in the above autobiographical incident.

B. In the space below, see if you can add any of the required elements of the prewriting guide which the author seemed to omit.

Magazine Magic *(cont.)*

Teacher Guide

Article Seven: *Event—Observation*

Students will write about an important and exciting event or place they have attended. Brainstorm about specific events, places, or activities that students have been to or would love to attend that could relate in some way to their magazines.

Possible Examples

- A surfboard competition
- A BMX competition
- A car or motorcycle show
- An N.B.A. playoff game
- The World Series
- The Academy Awards
- The Grammy Awards
- A Paris fashion show

- Working behind the scenes at a television or movie set
- Flying a 767 Boeing airplane
- Digging up an Egyptian tomb
- Participating in a music video
- Dancing on Broadway
- Discovering dinosaur bones on an archeological dig

Students need to hear some examples to figure out what would fit with their choice. If students have never participated in an event that is related to their theme, stimulate them to visualize and imagine what it would be like.

Distribute the event prewriting guide outline on page 130. Use the student samples on pages 131 and 132 to model an event. Show the students that past tense verbs are normally used throughout such a selection since the event has already occurred. Also, however, have them notice that a past event may be written about as if it were taking place right now. In this case, present tense verbs are used to convey a sense of action and immediacy. When this happens, we call it "using the *historical present*." "The Women's World Cup" on page 131 is an example of effective use of the historical present. It is important to be consistent and logical throughout the article in the tense use and sequence.

After students have read both samples (pages 131 and 132), ask them to respond to the challenge question on page 132. They are asked to list the verbs in each event observation and describe the major differences of writing style.

Use an overhead projector or the chalkboard to write a topic sentence on a selected theme.

Give multiple examples of past tense verb usage. Remind students that normally only past tense verbs should be used unless the historical present is chosen for the whole selection. Action verbs are an important component in this selection. Have students list past tense action verbs aloud and create a word bank on an overhead projector or the chalkboard. Suggest that the students make a list in their spiral notebooks of some past tense action verbs that could be used in their event article. The event should be written as a highlight of their life that will always be remembered.

Remind students to supply an original title for their event.

Magazine Magic *(cont.)*

Teacher Guide

Article Seven: *Event—Observation (cont.)*

Event—Observation Prewriting Guide

I. **Introduction:** Begin with a topic sentence that focuses on what you have experienced and witnessed as an observer, not as a participant. Identify the event and introduce it with a specific time and place.

    A. Where was the event?

    _____

    B. When was the event?

    _____

II. **The Body of the Event**

    A. Describe the event with action verbs.

    _____

    _____

    _____

    B. Describe how you felt being an observer in this important event.

    _____

    _____

    _____

III. **Conclusion**

    A. Why was this the significant event chosen?

    _____

    _____

    B. How did this event affect any future decisions about experiencing this event again?

    _____

    _____

Use this prewriting guide to expand into a multiple-paragraph observational event. Write the rough draft in your spiral notebook.

Article Seven: *Event—Observation* (cont.)

Student Sample #1: "Women's World Cup"

I have been waiting for this moment for almost a year now, and finally here I am at the U.S.A. Women's World Cup game. They are playing a very, very good team—China. At last, the game starts. I look around, and there must be at least 2,000 people screaming and yelling at the top of their lungs, rooting for both teams. As the game goes on, there is a close call when China gets a break-a-way shot, but it hits the post and goes out of bounds.

A few minutes later, Brandi Chastain takes it up the field and passes to Mia Hamm. Mia shoots and SCORES! GOAL! U.S.A. leads by one.

Now it is halftime, and the crowd cheers the players off the field. As time goes on, the crowd waits anxiously for the players to take the field again.

At last, the game starts up again, and—"UH OH," China is on another break-a-way. Briana Scurry slides to stop the ball, and accidentally kicks one of China's players, taking her down. Immediately, the referee blows his whistle to call a penalty shot against team U.S.A. A player from China named Kim Joug shoots to the left, hits the inside of the post, and it goes in. At this point, the crowd roars with excitement! I keep thinking to myself throughout the rest of the game, what a battle this has turned out to be! There must be at least ten breakaways without any points being scored.

There are 12 seconds left in the game, when all of a sudden, Mia Hamm takes a corner kick right across the goal. Michelle Akers heads the ball. Just as the ball is ready to go in, the referee blows his whistle, and the game is over. The crowd goes WILD!

Now, it is all up to a shoot-off. First, U.S.A. steps up, shoots, and scores. China then scores. The crowd stays silent with shock. Five more times in a row both teams score. Now it's China's turn and they miss. Still the crowd stays eerily quiet. It is up to Team U.S.A. If they score, they will win, and if they don't, they are tied again.

Brandi Chastain steps up, shoots, and scores! U.S.A. wins the World Cup! At last, the crowd goes wild!

Magazine Magic *(cont.)*

Teacher Guide

Article Seven: *Event—Observation (cont.)*

Student Sample #2: "Wow! What a Piece of Work!"

There are a lot of things that I have experienced, but one thing certainly takes the cake.

It was July 30, 1999, when I went to go visit my uncle, who's in the Air Force. That's when I found out that as a late birthday present, he was going to take me to the Britney Spears concert in Hollywood!

As soon as we entered the concert room, on July 31, 1999, I knew that it would be a blast. There were so many crazed fans, even a guy dressed up in an angel costume with feathered wings. There were also all kinds of posters, signs, and glow-in-the-dark sticks.

It was so exciting to see Britney Spears doing her kicking dance moves. Her special effects were incredibly outrageous, but cool. Although I'm not one of her extreme fans—one of those whose life revolves around her—I have to admit that her concert was the bomb and a bag of Doritos.

One of the greatest things about this event was the fact that I was lucky enough to go. I mean, some adults don't even get to go to concerts. Another reason I enjoyed this was because it was my first concert and worth the money spent. It was a blast, and I am so happy that I was able to experience this.

Challenge

A. List below the verbs used in student samples #1 and #2.

"Women's World Cup"	"Wow! What a Piece of Work!"

B. Describe the major differences in writing styles for each selection.

Magazine Magic *(cont.)*

Teacher Guide

Article Eight: *Play Script*

Students will write a one-act play that requires conflict and resolution. Explain to students that a one-act play takes place with only one scene, one setting, and in the same time period throughout the play. Give details stating that the significant difference between a play and a short story is that there is continual dialog (accompanied by stage directions) in a play, while a short story uses narrative development and description along with the dialog. As an example of play format, read the student sample on pages 134 and 135 to the class and display it on an overhead projector.

Students need to know that a script from a play does not require quotation marks. Explain that a short story can be made into a play by writing a script for the theater or film. Tell students that most often a scriptwriter is hired, not the original novelist, to write a screenplay from a novel.

Ask students if they have read a book first and afterward have seen a movie based on a book. *Where the Red Fern Grows* is a classic example. The students who have read the novel and have seen the movie will generally agree that the book was better than the movie. The students will usually show disappointment that the movie left out many parts they felt were important.

Whenever students compare a book with a movie, it is usually a good opportunity to offer a judgment, sharing with the class that the judgment is an evaluation. Promotion of reading is clearly strengthened when students use their evaluation techniques to support reading. Here is a time to point out the superiority and unparalleled power of reading to enable others to experience exactly what an author intended for the reader.

✦

Introduce the assignment by explaining that this play the students are to write may use several characters but requires only two characters who have a problem and must find a solution. Brainstorm about problems that could occur relating to any of the magazine themes. For example, the problem might be a competition: two competitors feel they both have won the race. How can this be resolved? Alternatively, two girls might be trying out for a modeling job, and one of them lies about her qualifications and gets the job. Should the other girl tell?

Have students think about what could happen now, a situation that must be solved immediately because it happens in one day—a one-act situation. Explain that the play action must be sequential (no flashbacks) with the absence of quotation marks.

✦

After the completion of the magazine, this play may be acted out by the author and chosen classmates or may be performed as a puppet play. In either case, students will be making all decisions on set, scenes, and characters or puppets. For a puppet presentation, a classroom table may be flipped over. The students sit on the floor behind the table. With construction paper, the students may design a thematic screen or window for the puppets. This screen can then be taped to the edge of the table. To avoid shuffling of papers, students can tape their script to the back of the table, where it is easy to read but invisible to the audience. Such a performance is usually performed quickly and can be a joy to watch. If equipment is available, the play may also be videotaped.

Magazine Magic *(cont.)*

Teacher Guide

Article Eight: *Play Script*

Student Sample of a Play: "Waiting for the Bus"

Cast	
The Girl:.	Ashleigh
The Girlfriend:.	Michelle
The Cute Boy #1:.	Brandon
The Cute Boy #2:.	Matt

Setting: *A street corner of the neighborhood, early one Friday morning while the girls are waiting to go to school.*

Michelle: Hey, Ashleigh, what are you planning to do after school today?

Ashleigh: I don't know yet; I haven't made any plans yet.

Michelle: I was thinking of going to the mall. Maybe we could find some cute guys to take us to the movies tonight.

(All of a sudden a hot-looking car comes driving by.)

Ashleigh: Hey, Michelle, did you see the two guys in that car!

Michelle: Yeah!

Ashleigh: They look kind of cute.

(The boys must have noticed the girls because the car turns around and comes back and stops in front of the girls.)

Brandon: Good morning, Ladies.

(The girls both begin to giggle.)

Magazine Magic *(cont.)*
Teacher Guide

Article Eight: *Play Script*

"Waiting for the Bus" *(cont.)*

Brandon: My name is Brandon, and this is my friend, Matt.

Matt: Hello.

Michelle: Hi!

Ashleigh: Hi, I'm Ashleigh, and this is my friend, Michelle.

Brandon: I don't think I've seen you at school.

(The girls get a little sillier, knowing that these boys must be from the high school, and that they would like to have dates for tonight.)

Ashleigh: Uh . . .no, I'm new to the neighborhood.

Matt: *(Asking Brandon)* Hey, Dude! Why don't we give these babes a ride to school?

Brandon: So girls—how about if we give you girls a ride to school?

Ashleigh: *(getting a little bit nervous)* Well, we're waiting for a friend.

Michelle: And they should be getting here any second now.

(Just then the big, yellow school bus pulls up and honks at the boys to get them to move out of the way.)

Brandon: We must be in the way.

Matt: Why don't we pull into the driveway?

(While the boys are moving the car out of the way, the girls turn and start running to get into the school bus.)

Michelle: *(with an embarrassed tone in her voice)* Bye, boys! We've got to go.

Ashleigh: We'll catch you later.

(on the bus now)

Michelle: I hope we can see them again.

Ashleigh: Yeah, but, do you really think that some cute guys from the high school would actually ask out two girls from the junior high?

Michelle: I don't know, but it sure would be fun!

Magazine Magic *(cont.)*

Teacher Guide

Some additional activities based on writing formats introduced earlier in the year may be added to the magazine to enrich its content and provide more practice in writing skills.

Advertisement

The students are to create or invent an original product that they may eat, wear, or use that relates to their magazine. They are then to write an ad for the product to appear in the magazine.

Explain that this product is so revolutionary that everyone who reads this magazine will want to buy this product immediately. This product will change history!

Ask students about the latest advertised products they have heard about or read. Inquire how this product was marketed: television, magazines, newspapers, videos, Internet, or through shopping at selected stores of interest.

Brainstorm for ideas. Have students combine products, making up something humorous that could be sold. For example, golfers might buy a golf ball that automatically bounces out of the cup and into the golfer's hand after the golfer has putted it into the cup. Another example might be to appeal to homeowners to buy grass seed, which after it grows a perfect height of one inch never has to be mowed by their teenagers.

- ❏ Encourage humor with the advertisement.

- ❏ The product may be filled with nonsense, or it may be totally realistic.

- ❏ The product needs an original name.

- ❏ The product must be priced.

- ❏ The product benefits need to be explained and promoted.

- ❏ Where can this product be purchased? May this product be purchased by a variety of ways?

- ❏ This product must be shown with a drawing or computer graphics.

- ❏ The size of the advertisement should cover at least one-half page of notebook paper.

- ❏ The advertisement must be colorful and immediately grab the attention of the reader.

- ❏ The student may create more than one advertisement.

Student samples for advertisements for three original products appear on page 137. They may be reproduced or placed on a transparency for use with an overhead projector.

Magazine Magic *(cont.)*
Teacher Guide

Student Samples of Advertisements

"Night Light Mirror"

Do you ever find yourself going out at night and want to touch up your makeup or hair, but you can't because it's too dark? Well, here's your solution—Night Light Mirror. It has lights all around the outside of the frame. It can be a lap or hand mirror. The handle folds in and out. Its handle folds in when you want it to be a lap mirror.

"Magic Carpet"

The newest and hottest item for every home is Magic Carpet. It's a carpet or rug with a hidden pocket in it for hiding candy, personal notes, letters, and money. It is basically a hiding place for anything that you don't want to be found!

What is the chance of somebody in your family looking inside a rug? This makes a great gift, at a reasonable price. It comes in a series of sizes, colors, and shapes. Get with the program and order now!

At all participating stores or call: 1-800-53-MAGIC

"Game-On Remote Control Goal"

Do you have back pains from carrying your goal out of the street every time a car passes by? Well, the Game-On Remote Control Goal is for all you street hockey fans. This goal has a battery and antenna built inside the crossbar. It also has a hand-held remote control that you can set on the sidewalk. This remote control will move the goal horizontally across the street, allowing cars to pass by. The cost is $75 for one, and $115 for two. You will only find this product at Ryan's Sporting Goods.

Magazine Magic *(cont.)*
Teacher Guide

Concrete Poem

The student will write a poem and then create a shape that represents the theme of both the poem and magazine. The students are to write the poem in stanza form first. Using the examples on page 139, have the students imagine what shape would best illustrate the concrete poems. Make an overhead of concrete poem samples, and draw a shape to show students the differences in the shapes and themes of these poems. Request additional shape suggestions from students that the poems may also illustrate.

Brainstorm examples of shapes that could be the subjects of concrete poems:

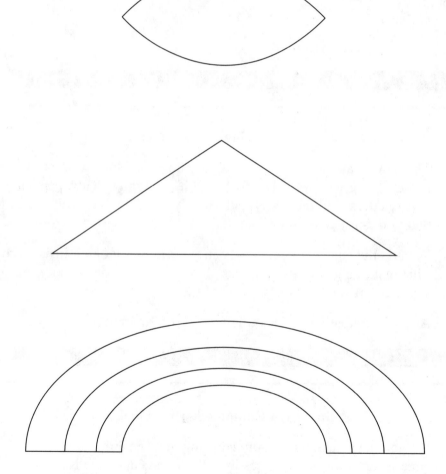

- Footballs
- Goal Posts
- Baseball Diamond
- Catcher's Mitts
- Ice-Cream Cones
- Rainbows
- Trucks
- Cars
- Car Parts
- Truck Parts
- Jewelry
- Hair Styles
- Sailboats
- Dogs
- Cats
- Lipstick Tubes
- Skirts
- Dresses
- Dinosaurs
- Egyptian Tombs
- Musical Notes
- Instruments
- Grammy Statue
- Oscar Statue

Students will write the poems in stanza form. Review with them that when writing a poem in stanza form, each line of poetry begins with a capital letter. Not all poems have complete sentences, but we still use punctuation marks when needed. Then demonstrate to students how to write their poems within the shape of the object they have drawn. Expect the use of vivid language to describe the object, especially action verbs and descriptive adjectives. Keep the thesaurus handy.

Use markers, crayons, or colored pencils to finish illustrating the shape. Both the stanza and the concrete poem must be written on the same page.

Magazine Magic *(cont.)*

Teacher Guide

Student Sample #1	Shape?
There was a boy named Alex Knight, His mom bought him a Game Boy Light, Alex played it all through the night. As he was playing Pokemon, The game suddenly sucked him up. Where was he? He could not tell, Until he saw a Weepinbell . . . A flash went through his head: Was he dead? Not at all, He was actually dreaming in his bed. And then it hit, He wasn't in a Pokemon world . . . Not for a year, A month, A day, Not even the slightest bit.	

Student Sample #2	Shape?
Lizzy wakes up every day, And hopes that she will get time to play. She's in math when the teacher says, "Today is the day for a quiz." She starts to think, "I'm dead meat!" When someone says, "You can cheat." She starts to say how it's wrong when she sees the test. "It's so long!" "It's not a good choice," Says a voice in her head. "It's a plan," says the little man. "But it's wrong!" she yelled in her head. "I would rather get my grade and go to bed." She gets her grade and she failed. Her teacher says it will be mailed. She goes home to tell her mother, But she'd rather tell another. She goes to ask her brother for advice, Then she realizes he's not very nice. She goes to her mother to tell her about the test, And can only hope for the best. Her mother understands how she was busy, But that's not like lazy. Since she told the truth, She could take the test over in a booth.	

Magazine Magic *(cont.)*
Teacher Guide

Compact Disc

Engage the students with a great opportunity to write lyrics to a song that relates to their magazine theme. These lyrics will fit into the clear CD case that they will be bringing to school. Not only are they going to write the lyrics to a song that relates to the theme of their magazine, but they will also design the front and back cover of their CD to match the magazine theme. Their compact disc case will be decorated with original artwork or a design that will cover both sides of the CD case. The students will measure and calculate the dimensions of a CD case and figure out how to make a template that would fit into their case. They should make two patterns, one for the front and back cover that will be folded as a book. The second pattern will be used for the actual lyrics. Students may also make a mock CD out of construction paper, cover it with aluminum foil, and name it.

Begin by asking how important music is to the student's life. Ask the students if they know that more than one person often writes the song. Explain that there are many song-writing teams. One person writes the melody or music, and one person writes the lyrics or the words. Of course, there are also musicians who can do both, plus perform what they have written. Enlighten the students by explaining that a song is a poem to music. Ask the students whether they read the enclosed lyrics in a CD case while the song is playing.

The lyrics should be at least two stanzas, four lines each. They may use the rhyme scheme of AABB, ABAB, or variations of these.

Student CD Sample

"Twinkle, Twinkle, Little Cat"
Twinkle, twinkle, little cat,
How I wonder where you're at.
Through the night I search and sigh,
Why, oh why, oh why, oh why?
Little, little, little cat,
How I wonder where you're at.
Where, oh where, could you have gone?
Please come back before the dawn.
Little cat, please come home.
I've been waiting so alone.
If you come, you'll find a treat,
Tuna fish and juicy meat.
In the distance walks a cat,
I see his stomach—empty, flat.
I notice him, so gaunt and blue,
looking sad, without a clue.

Magazine Magic *(cont.)*
Teacher Guide

News Broadcast

Collaboratively, students choose two or three class members and coordinate a brief news broadcast, using a favorite article chosen by each class member. This activity will be coordinated after the final copy of the entire magazine has been completed.

This may be an activity that students may want to work on if they have finished their final drafts more quickly than others. If this is the case and students have begun to hand in their magazines before the due date, privately explain the news broadcast. These motivated students make great peer tutors.

The news broadcast is very informal. The students may sit behind a table, construct a microphone, and share, not read, a favorite article they have written. Students must tell why they chose an article, using evaluation and stating judgments.

The broadcast team needs time to rehearse the production, deciding when each person speaks. Since most of the students have watched news broadcasts and talk shows, have them rehearse together for a five- to ten-minute performance. The students may need suggestions about how to use a transition as a cue to let the next newscaster begin to talk.

Ask the students how news broadcasters keep their broadcast moving smoothly. How do these people end their segments? Do they introduce the next person with a quick preview of what that broadcaster will be talking about? The students must know when it is their turn, use eye contact, and share one favorite article. Each person should talk about his article for about one or two minutes. In addition, each student may use any visuals he has created. Students may wish to explain a game they have invented or share ideas about a good book they have just read.

A "talk show" forum may also be used. Both girls and boys enjoy this style. One student may be the host or hostess and ask the other students about their favorite articles. The host or hostess may conclude the show by sharing his or her favorite article. If the students choose a talk show forum, it must be "G" rated and tasteful. Boys as well as girls also enjoy making a "sports talk show" presentation, using a variety of sports articles as one common theme. Any of these performances, of course, may be videotaped if equipment is available.

Selling the Magazine

Part of the broadcast may include students creating a sales pitch to sell the magazine.

Explain the importance of effective advertisement and marketing of products. Ask what strategies advertising agencies and companies are using now to market their products.

Students may answer: Internet, videos, TV, cable programs using infomercials, magazines, newspapers, radio, billboards, mail, door-to-door sales, and telemarketing.

Ask students to observe television commercial marketing of products to see if they can use any of the strategies to sell their magazine to the class.

- The students may write a short jingle, poem, or a "one-liner."
- The sales pitch may be either serious or humorous.
- The magazine must be brought up in front of the class as a prop.
- The students will make a creative presentation to persuade the class to buy the magazine.
- This activity will be presented as the students' final performance.

Magazine Magic *(cont.)*
Student Guide

Check-Off List

Name: _____

Date Due: _____

Materials: spiral notebook, pencils, pens, ruler, markers, construction paper, dictionary, thesaurus tagboard, colored pencils, crayons, compass.

Cover and Publication: The cover and the title of your magazine must be original. The cover is student choice. You may use construction paper or a commercial clear folder with your original design and artwork. The magazine may be word-processed or handwritten in ink.

Directions: Check off each item when completed. Glue this list inside your spiral notebook. Keep all articles in one spiral notebook. This will be your rough draft copy. All final copies will be done at home.

Table of Contents

Each page must be identified with a title of article or activity and corresponding page number. This will be done only after all the final drafts have been written. Each activity and article must have an original title. Do not use the title on the check-off list.

Activities

1. *Vocabulary:* Create a vocabulary activity that uses 15 or more vocabulary words that relate to the theme of your magazine. This activity may be a word search, crossword puzzle, word scramble, or a mystery/code puzzle. An answer key is required.

2. *Horoscope:* Using all twelve astrological signs, speculate about someone's life. What effect would this speculation have on a person's life? Provide only positive predictions. Try to relate these predictions to your magazine theme. The astrological signs are as follows: Aries (March 21–April 19), Taurus (April 20–May 20), Gemini (May 21–June 20), Cancer (June 21–July 22), Leo (July 23–August 22), Virgo (August 23–September 22), Libra (September 23–October 22), Scorpio (October 23–November 21), Sagittarius (November 22–December 21), Capricorn (December 22–January 19), Aquarius (January 20–February 18), Pisces (February 19–March 20).

3. *Jokes:* Write three jokes, riddles, or cartoons. You may choose any combination of the three. If you wish, you may add more. The jokes are not required to relate to the magazine, but they may.

4. *Song:* Write a song using a familiar tune like "Row, Row, Row Your Boat," and replace the lyrics with words which relate to your magazine. You may use any familiar tune. A five-line song should be the minimum. Also, create a musical instrument as an accompaniment. Combine familiar instruments together, and give it an original name. Draw this instrument, and include it with your song on the same page.

5. *Math Puzzle/Game:* Create a math game or puzzle. You may use challenging word or number problems, or create a visual game of logic. You may also create math graph art. Remember to include an answer key.

Magazine Magic *(cont.)*
Student Guide

Check-Off List *(cont.)*

Articles

1. *Short Story:* Write a fictitious account of a person(s), place(s), or event(s). You must show conflict between well-developed characters and the environment. Use at least ten lines of dialog. Use descriptive language. Develop the plot with logic and sequence. The story must have a resolution. The plot must relate to your magazine theme.

2. *Feature:* Write an article with facts, data, and modern research on a chosen subject. Concentrate on making this article newsworthy. This article is true. This article may focus on new products or inventions that have been designed or people who have made contributions to this magazine theme.

3. *Event:* Write about an important and exciting event or place to which you have traveled. Tell what you have remembered and convey the excitement that you felt when you thought back upon this experience. If you haven't traveled to this particular event, use your imagination and write about how this experience would be memorable. For example, this event may be a concert, a Paris fashion show, a spectacular sporting event, or a dinosaur dig.

4. *Advice Column:* Create four problems and respond with four solutions to the problems that you have written. Title this advice beginning with "Dear" (followed by the name of your magazine). Sign each problem with a fitting response. Use a "friendly" letter-writing format to answer each problem. The problems and solutions will relate to your magazine theme.

5. *Evaluation:* Evaluate a book. The book does not have to relate to your magazine theme. You must present a judgment on the worth of the book with reasons and evidence. Do not summarize the plot and events. Give reasons why you like, or do not like the book. Be specific and use supporting details and examples to back up your evaluation. Recommend this book to a specific audience, using both age group and interest.

6. *Interview:* Choose an important person who shares your interests about your magazine and write an interview, using a question-and-answer format. You must have ten questions and ten corresponding answers. All questions and answers must be in complete sentences.

7. *Autobiographical Piece:* Write about how you became involved with this interest, hobby, or subject. Explain about the specific events in your life that led up to this magazine choice. How old were you when you became interested in this topic? Who influenced you to pursue this interest? Will this interest carry through to a career choice? Have you influenced anyone else to become interested in this activity?

8. *Play Script:* Write a one-act play that requires a conflict and resolution. Provide the play with at least two characters. Prepare the play with dialogue, scenes, location, dates, stage directions, and costumes. Performance of this play is optional. This play should be at least two pages long.

Magazine Magic *(cont.)*

Student Guide

Check-Off List *(cont.)*

Articles

9. *News Broadcast:* Collaboratively choose at least three other class members, and coordinate a short news broadcast or "talk show" forum to share one or two of your favorite articles. This broadcast will be presented in front of the class, showing the variety of magazine themes written by other students.

10. *Advertisement:* Create and draw an original product that relates to your magazine. Name it, price it, and explain the benefits of buying it.

11. *Concrete Poem:* Write a concrete poem that depicts and creates a shape that is related to your magazine theme. The poem will outline the shape of the object chosen. Also, remember to write this poem in stanza form.

12. *Compact Disc:* Design an original front and back cover of your own clear CD case which you bring to class. Write an original poem that relates to the theme of your magazine. Your CD case must have original artwork as well as an original name that relates to your magazine theme.

13. *Selling the Magazine:* Create a sales pitch that would sell your magazine. It may be a short jingle, poem, or a "one-liner." You will sell your magazine to the class at the completion of this project.